SASQUATCH CANADA

BEYOND BRITISH COLUMBIA

W.T. WATSON

BEYOND THE FRAY

Publishing

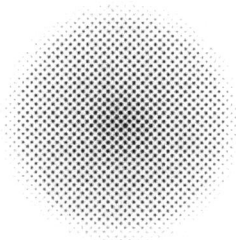

BEYOND THE FRAY

Publishing

There is your Big Man standing there, ever waiting, ever present like the coming of a new day. He is both spirit and real being, but he can also glide the forest like a moose with big antlers, as though the trees aren't there ... I know him as my brother ... I want him to touch me, just a touch, a blessing, something I could bring home to my sons and grandchildren, that I was there, that I approached him, and he touched me.

Lakota Elder Pete Catches, from In the Spirit of Crazy Horse *by Peter Mathiesson.*

INTRODUCTION

I started this project with some trepidation. One has only to spend some time listening to podcasts and consuming media about the legendary forest creature that I will refer to as Sasquatch to realize opinions about what these beings are vary wildly. In addition, those opinions can sometimes be accompanied by considerable rancour, and those who do not agree with certain thinking can be subjected to vitriol from those who hold the "correct" beliefs.

Still, as I did the research for my book *Canadian Monsters and Mysteries*, I realized that when Sasquatch in Canada was discussed, with a few notable exceptions, the attention of researchers veered toward British Columbia (BC).

I certainly understand this bias. BC is connected to the great Pacific Northwest wilderness where these creatures are often seen, and there is a rich community of researchers actively engaged in the hunt for Sasquatch there even as I write this. As I commented in *Canadian Monsters and Mysteries*, however, Canada is the second-largest country in the world. While BC is not a small province, it is literally possible to hide whole countries in the vastness of the Canadian wilds stretching from the borders of BC all the way to the Atlantic coast. I decided that I would focus my research on the areas outside of British Columbia so that persons interested in Sasquatch could see the wide variety of sightings across the breadth of this huge country.

And Canada is huge, as I pointed out above, though the vast majority of the Canadian population lives within 150 miles of the US border. If I drive two hours from my home, I can be in forested areas that stretch unbroken to meet the Arctic tundra. A few hardy souls and First Nations people inhabit these gigantic swathes of wilderness. It is an ideal location for a large, undiscovered creature to live.

And, in fact, Canada is home to a Lazarus species—a species that is supposed to have gone extinct, only to be rediscovered later. Canada's Lazarus species is the wood bison, the largest land animal in North American. The wood bison is supposed to have gone extinct in the early part of the twentieth century due to disease and overhunting, but in 1957, the species was rediscovered by a Canadian wildlife officer as he was making an overflight of a wilderness area in Alberta.

If the largest known land animal in North America can hide out in the Canadian forest for a few decades without being seen, imagine what a determined and intelligent Sasquatch might do.

I chose the quote from Pete Catches, a Lakota (Sioux) medicine person, that opens this book for a reason. My feelings about Sasquatch are very ambivalent.

On the one hand, I am perfectly willing to entertain the idea that there may be an undiscovered species of great ape or hominid living in the wilds of North America and beyond. However, one has only to read books like Timothy Renner and Joshua Cutchin's *Where the Footprints End* series to suspect that something far stranger is going on, at least in some cases.

I've struggled with this strangeness that surrounds the Big Man, as some indigenous people call the creature, since I was a sixth grader reading Ivan Sanderson's epic work on the Abominable Snowman. Even though Sanderson presented the evidence and made the argument that the "Abominable Snowman" was a flesh and blood creature that lived all over the world, I had an intuitive feeling of strangeness about what I came to think of as Sasquatch. I had no doubt that it existed—there were far too many witnesses to ignore—but I wondered, along with all the skeptics, why it was that no firm physical evidence had been found for that existence.

That feeling persisted, much later, when I began to look at the stories of Sasquatch in Canada. While the vast majority of sightings in the Great White North seem to be of a flesh and blood creature, there are still aspects of some cases that seem to indicate that we are dealing with something more than a flesh and blood animal.

I have chosen not to make this book a massive compendium of every sighting I could find in my research. Accordingly, I will open with several sections in which I detail sightings in Alberta, Manitoba, Ontario, and other provinces of Canada.

Once I have laid out a wide assortment of sightings stretching across the wilderness of the Great White North, I will dive into more specific areas of Sasquatch research. As an example, I have chosen to focus on visual sightings even though many people believe they have come into contact with Sasquatch because of wood knocks, vocalizations, stone throwing and the like. Those experiencers were simply too numerous for me to include in the book, but I will devote a section to discussing this secondary evidence and an alternative theory for the many convincing but nonvisual encounters.

I will also discuss the beliefs of some of the First Nations people about Sasquatch. In that discussion, I will stray outside the borders of Canada to examine statements from indigenous people in the States. The reason for this is simple practicality.

Native people, for the most part, are quite reluctant to discuss these creatures, so I had to cast the net a little wider to find pertinent data. I think that the opinions of First Nations people are very relevant to this topic and may open our minds to the true nature of this phenomenon.

Following this template, I hope to produce a work that will provide those interested in Sasquatch with a wide variety of sighting information—the major argument for a flesh and blood creature (usually)—as well as ideas and concepts that may argue for something far stranger existing in the woods of Canada. Because they are so common, I have included a chapter on road-side and road crossing sightings with some thoughts about highways, byways, and liminality.

One area that I have avoided is discussion of the numerous photos and videos online. I do not pretend to have expertise in the realm of photo or video analysis, and unlike many who claim such expertise after an hour online, I will stay out of these arguments in order to avoid getting bogged down in the endless arguments—pro and con—raging around the photographic and film evidence available. While these videos and pictures add to the mass of circumstantial evidence that surrounds this subject, in this age of image manipulation, it is impossible to accept them as conclusive proof.

Finally, I will conclude the book with some interesting cases that I kept in a file called "weird stuff" (the file had a much more scatological name, but I am editing for language). Even though it seems that most witnesses are seeing an animal or hominid of some sort, the weird-stuff cases should cause the reader to think about the actual nature of this being.

Anyone who has read this far will note that I have not used the term "Bigfoot" to refer to these beings. The word Sasquatch, according to Kristi Lane Sinclair, a Haida/Cree indigenous filmmaker, derives from a Sts'ailes (Chehalis) word—Sa:sq'ets—

which means wild man. The word Sasquatch was coined as an Anglicization of the Sts'ailes word by John Burns, a teacher on the Chehalis reserve. I will generally refer to the creatures by this name or one of the other indigenous referents, such as the Big Man or Hairy One, since I feel, along with Native people, that these majestic beings, whatever they are, are deserving of respect.

Now, let us move on to the great province of Alberta for our first experiences of the Canadian Sasquatch outside of British Columbia.

CHAPTER ONE
ALBERTA

I CHOSE to begin our tour of Sasquatch sightings in Alberta for two reasons. One is that I am inclined to organize things alphabetically when I can. The other is that there is a richness of data to work from, including a whole book written by veteran Sasquatch researcher Thomas Steenburg. Additionally, the Alberta Sasquatch organization maintains a database of sightings, as does the better-known Bigfoot Field Researchers Organization. Finally, I also found extensive sighting information in newspapers and online articles, all of which demonstrate that Alberta is an active Sasquatch area.

Wikipedia tells us that Alberta is the fourth-largest Canadian province at 661,848 square kilometres (255,541 square miles). The region is extremely diverse, with the northern half of the province covered by boreal forest, while the southwestern boundary is occupied by the Rocky Mountains and their densely forested foothills. In the southeast, one finds a range of prairie environments as well as the so-called badlands, deep canyons from which a number of dinosaur fossils have been retrieved.

As you might expect, the woodlands are home to an astonishing variety of animals, including several large predators, including wolves, grizzly bears, black bears, and mountain lions. From a purely biological viewpoint, if grizzly bears, which can weigh up to 790 pounds, can survive in the wilds of Alberta, then it seems possible that a creature as large as the Sasquatch could do so as well.

David Childress, in his book *Bigfoot Nation: The History of Sasquatch in North America*, gives us the story of one of the earliest Sasquatch encounters in the region.

David Thompson was a British fur trader and explorer who came across strange tracks while walking in an area around what is now Jasper, Alberta. The find was so odd that he recorded it in his diary:

> I now recur to what I have already noticed in the early part of last winter, when proceeding up the Athabasca River ... we came to the track of a large animal, which measured fourteen inches in length by eight inches in breadth by a tape line. As the snow was about six inches in depth the track was well defined, and we could see it for a full hundred yards from us, this animal was proceeding from north to south. We did not attempt to follow it, we had not the time for it, and the Hunters, eager as they are to follow and shoot every animal, made no attempt to follow this beast, for what could the balls of our fowling guns do against such an animal ... the sight of the track of that large a beast staggered me, and I often thought of it, yet never could bring myself to believe such an animal existed, but thought it might be the track of some Monster Bear.

I find this account interesting since it gives us insight into the mind of a witness (of sorts). Thompson states that the creature the tracks belonged to was known to the local people, but he always thought that the reports were the result of people's "fondness for the marvellous". It was only upon seeing the gigantic tracks that Thompson was forced to admit that such a creature might just exist, even though he preferred to think that it must simply have been a "Monster Bear".

As we walk through the encounters in this book, we will find quite a number from hunters, hikers, and campers. One wonders how many of those people have seen something they couldn't explain and simply decided that it must have been a "Monster Bear".

While we are on the subject of bears, grizzlies, the largest bears in the region, leave a hind foot track that can range up to eleven inches long and seven inches wide, according to bear-tracker.com. The track that Thompson found was three inches longer than this and one inch wider, so it is possible that the trader found a giant bear track. What argues against this, though, is that Thompson makes no mention of the claw marks that would accompany the track of such a bear.

Sean Viala, mentioned more than once in my previous books, gives us a historical account in an article from the *SasquatchCanada Virtual Magazine*.

Lake Minnewanka is located in the Banff National Park in Alberta and was the site of an ongoing series of Sasquatch reports in the late 1800s. In 1895, several locals out fishing discovered a track of "gargantuan size" measuring over nineteen inches in length. This find was followed by another, in the winter of 1896, where tracks of a similar size were noted in the snow along the lakeshore. The individual who found the tracks followed them out onto the lake, where a hole had been broken in the ice. This person broke off his tracking when the trail disappeared into the woods.

In late spring of 1896, a trapper out checking his lines saw a large figure moving in the distance. He stated that the creature walked into the woods and had to duck to avoid a tree limb in its path. When the trapper later measured the height of the limb, it was over seven feet from the ground, indicating that whatever he saw was well over seven feet in height.

Two prospectors spotted what they assumed was a large bear in the late summer of 1896 and, being armed, fired on the creature. They were horrified when the animal stood up on two legs and shrieked at them before disappearing into the forest. The two departed with all due haste, and the creature was still shrieking in the woods as they made their retreat.

A similar incident occurred in the early winter of 1897 when, alerted by the barking of dogs, a group of men armed themselves and went out to confront the creature. When the animal was spotted, they opened fire on it, but, once again, it retreated into the woods, screaming as it went.

In 1897, two boys spotted the creature walking along a ridge, and then in fall 1898, a fisherman indulging in his pastime encountered the animal at a range of forty or fifty yards. Again, the human opened fire on what Viala feels was a Sasquatch, and again, the creature disappeared into the forest, emitting "hair raising cries". The fisherman thought he might have hit the beast since blood spatters were found in the area.

The creature just could not seem to stay away from the settlers. In the early winter of 1898, two Irish wolfhounds were found dead, and massive tracks were found in the vicinity and then in spring of 1899, the Sasquatch was sighted again. The creature was seen watching a pair of horses in the corral, and once more, the owner of the cabin where the animal was seen opened fire on the creature, claiming that he hit it three times. The beast fell down but then got back up and made a quick getaway into the woods.

The final sighting of the being in that area occurred in early winter of 1899 as a man on horseback spotted the creature "at a distance". The animal appeared to have a "bad limp" as it walked to the west, and Viala conjectures that this might have been the result of being shot so many times.

In any event, the Sasquatch was not seen in the area again. Given the trigger-happy reaction of the settlers to the creature's presence, I wouldn't blame any creature of the forest for vacating the area.

IN AN ARTICLE TITLED "SASQUATCH REPORTED, 44 Years Later", the Edmonton *Journal* gives us the details of another historical sighting. Oda Sneider's 1938 encounter occurred near her home thirty-five miles southwest of Rocky Mountain House.

Sneider and her eight siblings were walking the half mile to milk the cows when they spotted something strange. Along the way stood an abandoned log cabin, and on the roof of the cabin, a figure could be seen. Sneider was only eight at the time of the sighting, but she recalls vividly seeing a creature, over six feet tall, covered in brown fur with human-type hands and feet.

The children, thinking the animal was one of their brothers wearing their mother's muskrat coat, started to yell and run at the creature. Sneider says that the "monkey-faced" animal seemed puzzled by their behaviour and "scrambled" across the roof of the cabin before "ambling" off toward the nearby river.

Later, when the children cornered their brother, he swore that it was not him, and they realized that they had seen something unusual. One might dismiss this sighting, given the age of the witness at the time, but I think this would be a mistake. The article notes that Ms. Sneider and her family survived the "hungry thirties" (presumably due to the Great Depression) by "living off the land". People, even young people, who find themselves in that situation learn a great deal about their local wildlife since it may mean the difference between eating and not.

Such a witness will not mistake a bear or other animal for something more unusual, and bears, the most often-cited animal to be misidentified as a Sasquatch, do not make a habit of climbing on the roofs of houses.

———

PERHAPS THE BEST-KNOWN sighting of Sasquatch in Alberta occurred on 23 August 1969 (some reports say 24 August). Multiple authors have documented this episode, but I will be following Don Hunter and René Dahinden's *Sasquatch* and Thomas Steenburg's *Sasquatch in Alberta.*

At the time of the sighting, Big Horn Dam was under construction. The site was just west of the Alberta community of Nordegg on the North Saskatchewan River. Five men— Harley and Stan Peterson, Floyd Engel, Guy L'Hereux and Dale Boddy—were working on the foundation of a water pumping station when they noticed a figure on a ridge opposite them. They observed the being walking, then sitting and then walking again over a period of about forty-five minutes.

The witnesses described the creature as looking like a very large man with its head bent forward and "very hefty". Witness Boddy insisted that no bear could have walked as far or as long as this creature did on two legs. In addition, he stated that it was too tall and thin to be a bear.

The Sasquatch was about a half mile away, and the men did not have the benefit of binoculars or a camera to help gather details or document their sighting. The experience was enough, however, to make two of the men go up on the ridge while their comrades observed. Extrapolating from the height of their fellow workers and the trees on the ridge, the group estimated the height of the creature at somewhere around fifteen feet!

This height is outside the range that most researchers will accept. I find it fascinating that people who are perfectly willing to believe that an unknown species of great ape or hominid lives in the wilds of North America refuse to believe that the creatures could be much more than eight to ten feet tall and, indeed, work actively to debunk such height estimates. Hunter and Dahinden developed an elaborate theory to "explain" the "mistake" in the height estimate, but I will leave it to the reader to believe or not.

While I find his approach to the height question quite silly, Dahinden did play it smart when he hired on with the construction crew and gathered reports from the local Native people who were working on the dam. When they found out about his interest, he began to get confirmation from the locals that the creature was familiar to them. In fact, when they were shown the Patterson-Gimlin film, which seems to show a female Sasquatch in the forests of Northern California, they commented that "their" creature was not as massive and hairy as the one in the film. Additionally, "their" creature was much taller.

Of course, once the press got hold of the story, more witnesses came forward. Mark Yellowbird, a Cree person, described 14.5-inch tracks with a stride length of six feet. Yellowbird's daughter, Edith, along with three other Native women, sighted four of the creatures "working at something" adjacent to the David Thompson Highway.

Alec Shortneck, another worker at the dam, spotted one of the creatures as he was clearing brush for the construction. The animal was no more than fifty yards away from him, and he reported being so stunned that he just kept on clearing brush until the Sasquatch walked away.

It was further reported that a band of First Nations people under Chief Joseph Smallboys was travelling between Banff National Park and Nordegg during the time of the sightings. Several of the tribal members reported up-close visual contact with Sasquatch in that area in the spring and summer of 1969.

Steenburg notes that not all the First Nations people of the area were in accord with the building of the dam and that at least one enterprising reporter proposed that the creature was a manifestation of "Indian magic". Steenburg takes a more practical approach and wonders if the whole episode wasn't a hoax designed to halt the building.

While I am willing to entertain the "Indian magic" hypothesis and will speak more on such things later, I seriously doubt the hoax scenario. The wheels of "progress" are hard to stop once they are turning and money and jobs are on the line. I think that the witnesses and Native people of the area would have had to produce a Sasquatch and proven that it was endangered to halt the building of the dam.

As I have noted, this sighting is but one of many in Alberta, so let's move on.

———

THOMAS STEENBURG, in his excellent *Sasquatch in Alberta*, gives us the story of Debra Malone, which occurs near Abraham Lake, a body of water just south of the Big Horn Dam. In fact, Debra and her family drove past the dam construction site on their way to a family camping trip in the region.

After passing the dam construction, they continued for forty miles on the highway, then turned and took a forestry road twenty miles back into the bush. They stopped and set up camp in an area dense with trees and berry bushes, a plant type that we will see throughout the book.

Once camp was set up, Debra, then thirteen, found herself bored and decided to make an exploratory hike into the woods. She wandered for some time through "the natural mazes of tall pines and wildflowers" before stopping at a berry bush to pick some of the ripe fruit. It was then that she noticed an unusual odour in the air. It was "not as bitter as a skunk smell but muskier than a dog in heat", and as she took in the scent, Debra had a very clear feeling that she was not alone.

The witness spun around, dropping into a sort of half squat, and spotted an unknown creature approximately fifty feet away. She described the animal as eight feet tall and hairy with a "perfectly upright human posture". Its arms fell to well past its knees, and Debra stated that the shoulders were at least three feet across. The creature had "long, matted, dirty brown and grey hair" and a nose that jutted out from the face like "a flattened ball of putty".

The being simply stood there, staring at the witness with slate black eyes, while she tried to figure out what it was. Remember, this was 1972, and the Sasquatch was not nearly as well known as it is these days.

Debra and the Sasquatch stood watching each other for something like ten minutes. The creature did not move at all, nor did it show any signs of discomfort at her presence. Eventually, the Hairy One let out a "deep throaty moan", and it seemed that the sound released Debra from an almost trancelike state. She fled the scene but had to stop when nausea overtook her, and she paused to lose the contents of her stomach.

Debra made it back to camp without incident, but when she emerged from the trees, she was pale, reeked from vomiting and had tear tracks down her face. Something had obviously scared the poor girl half senseless, but, as so often happens in youth sightings, her mother simply discarded her description and told her she had seen a bear.

━━

DEBRA'S EXPERIENCE is one example of why Sasquatch witnesses are so reluctant to come forward or provide any identifying information. A story from the Edmonton *Journal* entitled "Is It a Great Hairy Beast or Myth that Won't Die?" provides another terrific example of why this is so.

The anonymous witness was driving through a "cut in the rock in the foothills west of Red Deer" in the summer of 1974. He rounded a curve and stopped dead as he spied "two huge, hairy creatures" in the road before him. The witness testified that he was thirty feet or so from the animals and conjectured that since he was coming from upwind, they may not have heard or smelt him coming.

The witness, a hunter and fisherman, had been into this country frequently and stated that he would be happy to go back into the woods. He was quoted as saying that "I'd like to see them again and get pictures of them. I don't think people need to fear them". The anonymous man further stated that he did not feel he could shoot a Sasquatch. He noted that they were "too human to shoot".

Unfortunately, the actual humans that this witness encountered were not as gentle as the Sasquatch he witnessed. The *Journal* article is attributed to the witness anonymously since he refused to have his name printed. Apparently, after his sighting, news of the event leaked out, and the witness was subjected to "three months of pure hell ... some people even threatened to bomb my home".

Accordingly, the witness noted that he would only give his full identification to scientists who were seriously investigating the phenomenon. The man further said, like many Sasquatch witnesses, that there should be a "massive, well-funded scientific search for and study of the Sasquatch".

I'm not sure what such a search might yield, but I would be interested in seeing modern science take a crack at this difficult subject.

1974 seems to have been a banner year for turning a corner in the road and running into a Sasquatch. In an article in the Red Deer *Advocate*, forty-two-year-old Ron Gummell of Calgary tells of an experience similar to the anonymous witness above.

Mr. Gummell had been a skeptic up to the time of his encounter, but the shock of encountering two Sasquatch creatures that he estimated at twelve feet tall was enough to make him change his mind. He is quoted as saying, "They were so big they could have picked my car up and thrown it into the lake."

The creatures were awesomely tall, massive and "covered with hair". In addition, Gummell noted that they had flat faces. As soon as they spotted his vehicle, they "sauntered into the bush".

I find this sighting interesting in that the creatures described are quite a lot taller than the "average" reported Sasquatch. Note that Abraham Lake is about twenty kilometres from the site of another giant Sasquatch sighting at Big Horn Dam, and Debra Malone's sighting happened in this area as well. Those who investigated the Big Horn Dam case and the sightings that were reported afterward wondered if there weren't a clan of giant Sasquatch in the area. Interestingly, Thomas Steenburg noted that the giant Sasquatch sightings in that area ceased after about 1984.

―――――

CURT NELSON, of *SasqatchCanada*, reported a very interesting Sasquatch sighting that occurred in 1979. Intriguingly, the article that documented this sighting was a result of follow-up that Nelson did on the Lake Minnewanka rash of historical sightings we spoke of earlier.

In August 1979, Raymond Lee and his friend Dave (no last name given) were hiking in the Banff area. Raymond told Curt Nelson the following story.

The time was 2200 hours, and the pair had come upon a meadow lit by the post-sunset afterglow. There was a stream to their left, and from that direction, they heard a whistling noise followed by what seemed to be footsteps moving from left to right.

As so often happens in these encounters, the sounds in the bush indicated to the friends that something large, such as an elk, was about to break cover. Imagine their surprise when six-to-seven-foot "dark creatures walking on two legs" appeared not more than forty feet away.

The witness noted that the creature did not seem to have a neck and that its head rested directly on its shoulders. The being walked by in right profile with its arms hanging down past its knees. Lee stated that the creature seemed slender to him, with long legs. As noted, this creature was dark, but Lee spotted a lighter-coloured patch on one of its ankles.

What Lee didn't know until later was that his friend Dave was watching a completely different creature as Lee was watching the dark Sasquatch. Dave later described his animal as a dirty white color, and it seems that Dave's creature was much heftier than the one spotted by Lee. Dave estimated the being's height at seven feet or more.

Both animals seemed to be headed for the same grove of trees. Dave stated later that, mostly, he was looking at the back of the lighter-coloured creature. Both witnesses stated that the creatures moved with definite purpose, as though they wanted to be out of there.

After observing the creatures, both friends wanted nothing

more than to be away and vacated the area quickly. This is a behaviour we will see repeatedly in these pages, so it is wise to take note of it now.

Curt Nelson, the writer of the article, notes that the drawing Raymond made of the creature he saw takes the idea of Sasquatch having no neck to an extreme. The being that Raymond drew was quite frightening looking, and Nelson draws comparisons between Raymond's illustration and pictures taken of an alleged Sasquatch by Cliff Crook in Washington state on 11 July 1995.

Nelson goes on to wonder if the being that Raymond saw wasn't a very aged Sasquatch with a spinal deformity. Nelson also mentions one of the great mysteries of Sasquatch research, the idea that there seem to be different types of these creatures, such as animals with three-, four- or five-toed tracks in evidence. We will return to that idea as we go along, but, in the meantime, what did Raymond Lee and Dave see? Did the two young men chance upon two Sasquatch wandering in the same direction, or do we have one of those odd perceptual stories where two witnesses see entirely different things?

I'VE SPOKEN in my other books about the skeptic's triad—the belief that those who encounter the unusual are either mistaken, deluded, or engaged in a hoax. However, when a former Canadian Forces member who served as a special operations soldier tells you he has seen one of these creatures and that the event occurred while he was serving and in the presence of other army personnel, then I think it is time for the so-called skeptics to hush and listen to the witness.

This veteran of fifteen years of service had two encounters, one involving "chatter", which occurred in Ontario and will be discussed in that section, and the other a visual sighting in Alberta. This soldier's testimony is recorded on the *Alberta Sasquatch* website, report #066.

In May 1983, the witness was in the area of Wainwright, Alberta, on a training mission. The entire brigade had located to the area, and this service member also had a specialization in electronics, so he and his partner were dispatched on a repair. The only information that the two had on the equipment that needed repair were the map coordinates. In those days before GPS, the pair were using a topographic map and the stated coordinates to try to locate the equipment.

The two soldiers stopped their camouflaged pickup truck on the side of the road, completely unfolding their map, and while one of them looked for the coordinates, the witness was watching a deer in a fire break approximately thirty to forty metres ahead at about eleven o'clock. Just as the witness was about to tell his partner to take a look at the deer, he saw something exit the tree line at high speed.

The soldier compared the size of the creature with the deer and concluded that it was about seven and a half to eight feet tall and easily four feet wide. It was huge, "built like a football player", and he could see "the hair flow in the air and bounce around as it was running". The hair was longer on the head than on the body, and the head appeared to be "pointed".

The witness continued to watch as the dramatic events unfolded.

[Translated from French by a Quebec researcher] He came from behind the deer, and when he got close, he put his hand on its head. At the same time, he put his other hand on the deer's neck and rotated on himself. So what happened is that the deer's body was held still while the head was twisted 180 degrees. He broke its neck on the spot ... and, in one fell swoop, he made a U-turn and kept running towards the woods ... while at the same time, grabbing the deer and swinging it over his shoulder ... and goodbye, we're gone. This was done in a split second.

The witness noted that a deer that size would weigh in the one hundred to two hundred pound range, so the animal was incredibly strong to pick this deer up and run away with it. Not only was the being strong, but the soldier, who had observed cheetahs running down gazelle in Africa, compared the speed of this animal to that of a cheetah.

Upon further questioning, the witness stated that the Sasquatch was brown but seemed to have some reddish tips to its hair or fur. He also observed that the creature started off leaping on all fours before moving to a bipedal stance for the kill. Also clearly observed was the fact that this being had hands, not paws.

The soldier was impressed by the sheer physicality of the Sasquatch. The animal was "V-shaped" like a body builder, and the witness could see its muscles working as it moved. He reiterated that the creature never slowed down as it took the deer and that the hunt was accomplished in "one, single fluid motion".

The witness was adamant that "to me, this was an animal that was effective at doing its job ... it's a predator, a hunter ... what it was doing was all planned and calculated ... and was practiced and repeated several times, over many years".

This testimony is so compelling that I think it stands on its own. I will only say that we learn, in his testimony, that this soldier not only served with the forces in Canada, but he also had experience hunting deer with a bow. This witness simply cannot be ignored.

ALLEX MICHAEL, writing in a periodical called *Animal Watch* and quoted in a Bigfoot Encounters article, tells the story of her harrowing sighting in Bow Valley Provincial Park in the summer of her sixteenth year. She had been working as a counsellor at an arts and crafts camp, and the job was complete. She had contacted her mother to come get her and a fairly large trunk of her possessions.

Michael stated that the summer had been pretty wild and that she had been one of the "sleep deprived party wimps" who had chosen not to stay in a cabin but had, instead, constructed a single-mattress-sized platform covered in poly-plastic as her sleeping area. Her makeshift sleeping quarters were about a fifteen-minute walk into the woods from the main camping area.

After a challenging drive into the camp area, the witness, her mother, and a small dog named Willow found themselves preparing to hike out to Michael's sleeping area to retrieve her belongings. The time was 0300 hours, a fact that Michael explained with a few reasons, including her family's propensity for doing things at odd hours.

The witness' mother pulled up to the now-deserted camp-site. All the campers had left some time earlier, and any permanent staff were either on days off or asleep in their cabins. The car headlights were left on as the three sorted themselves out for the short hike.

In another notable precursor to a Sasquatch sighting, the dog, Willow, firmly refused to leave the vehicle, instead hiding partially under the driver's seat. The mother and daughter shrugged this off and, leaving the dog in the car, began to journey into the woods.

Although they had a flashlight, Michael had issues finding the exact spot of her sleeping arrangement. What should have taken fifteen minutes ended up being a "30 minutes skin-scraping bushwhack". The witness assured her mother, once they arrived, that all that needed to be done was to take down the plastic cover and remove the mattress and her trunk. They would need two trips but should be able to accomplish the task in short order.

As the mother was reaching up to untie some knotted twine in the tree, the area flooded with a "pungent smell". Michael describes the encounter at that moment:

> There, distorted through the semi-transparent poly was a huge shadow only about 7 feet (2m) away. With the four-foot platform and me kneeling on top, the creature was easily at eye level. A split second later, there was an incredibly loud screaming roar. Although I know of nothing to describe it, the sound was like a peacock scream, a bear growl, and a lion roar all somehow combined ...

Whatever it was finally turned and walked slowly away on its long hind feet. We continued watching as each heavy step could be heard contracting [sic] the ground. There were no visible ears, just a sparse "Mohawk" like fringe sprouting up from the tapering top of the creature's head. From behind, the upper body appeared massive. It continued to walk upright until disappearing into the trees.

What should have taken two trips took the frightened duo one trip, as Michael clearly recalls "power-walking" away from the site with the mattress on her head and one handle of the trunk in her hand. Presumably, her mother carried the other end of the trunk.

The dog, when they arrived back at their vehicle, was still cowering under the front seat of the car, and the witness reported that she and her mother had a "very quiet drive home". While Michael did not state unequivocally that she had encountered a Sasquatch, she does go through a litany that will be familiar to anyone who has read even one text on the subject.

Michael allowed that there were brown bears in the area but notes that she had never seen a bear walk on its hind legs for the length of time that she observed, nor would a bear's gait have been that smooth. She also raised the question of whether she and her mother could have encountered a very large (over seven feet tall) furry "man" that night. She does not seem to believe this since she goes on to conjecture that the creature was a Sasquatch.

Given the description of the critter and the horrendous sound that it made, it seems likely to me that the witness encountered a Sasquatch at very close range. It is very difficult for the human animal to accept that it has seen something that it cannot immediately categorize, and Michael's attempts to relate her sighting to something more mundane are a classic example of this tendency.

A STORY from Thomas Steenburg's book on the Sasquatch in Alberta also takes place in the Bow Valley Provincial Park, a site near the camp where Allex Michael had her experience. This event occurred in May 2011 as the witness, whom Steenburg designated AV, was enjoying some time camping.

AV had been doing "typical camping things" through the day, and after dinner, he and a companion (not named) decided to go for a walk down along the Bow River. The walkers wandered down along the shoreline "not paying much attention to anything". The sun was beginning to set behind the mountains, so the group decided to head back to camp. AV took his dog down to the edge of the river, presumably to get a drink. The canine alerted, staring across the river.

At first, AV didn't see anything. The dog refused to move, and after a moment, the hair along her back began to stand on end. Given the dog's reaction, AV wisely stood over the canine and put his head down close to hers, hoping to see what was disturbing the animal.

AV noticed a "large mass across the river" at a range of about one hundred fifty to one hundred thirty yards. At first, he assumed that it was a large bear or, perhaps, a rock. After watching for thirty seconds or so, AV looked down and told the dog to come along.

When he looked up, AV was shocked to see that the creature had stood up. AV described the creature as dark but not black, likening it to a dun-coloured greyhound, a mixture of grey with some brown mixed in. It took a step to its left and then three more steps into the treeline, where it "blended so well with the shadows of the trees" that he lost sight of it.

AV could not be certain whether the being he spotted was hair covered or not, but he noted that it remained on two legs once it stood up and that it would have been seven to seven and a half feet tall with an estimated weight of "easily" five hundred pounds. AV, a former member of the Canadian Forces, stated that the figure was much larger than a soldier in full one-hundred-thirty-pound kit.

Steenburg notes that the creature seemed to stay completely still until AV broke eye contact to pay attention to his dog. As soon as AV was no longer looking directly at it, it appeared that the creature stood and walked away quickly. This certainly seems to indicate superior intelligence.

I am also interested in the dog's reaction to the beast. The Michael incident, which happened near Bow Valley, also involved a dog. In that case the canine refused to even exit the car when her two humans tramped off into the bush looking for Michael's campsite. I've read and heard of other Sasquatch encounters where dogs were involved, and almost universally, the canine species seems to have a healthy fear or at least respect for these forest giants.

I believe that if I were camping with my two dogs in Sasquatch country, I would keep a careful eye on my canine companions. It is certainly true that any alerts they might have are more likely to be related to bunnies and squirrels than they are to Sasquatch, but one never knows.

Steenburg, in *Sasquatch in Alberta*, also gives us the story of a witness who wished to remain anonymous but who encountered a Sasquatch in Jasper National Park.

The witness, whom Steenburg called William, was hiking with another person early in the morning of 17 August 1993. The first indication that something was not quite right happened when the two hikers heard a "strange hooting type noise" about thirty metres off the trail. Steenburg later played a recording alleged to be sounds made by the Fouke Monster in Arkansas, another Sasquatch-type being that became famous after the movie *Legend of Boggy Creek,* and the witness stated they were identical to what he and his hiking companion heard.

Curious, the pair went to investigate and were astonished to see a "large hairy man". William described the "man" as being about nine feet tall and "built bigger than a gorilla". The creature "appeared to be looking at something or someone", and when it noticed the two hikers, it turned to look at them. William stated that its eyes had "a gleam of intelligence and wild fury".

The two men fled with the creature close behind. The pair ran for about twenty minutes, and though they were certain the creature could have caught them, it did not. Instead, it simply seemed to be chasing them out of its area.

Eight hours later, the two worked up the nerve to return to the area and found footprints sunk three inches into the semi-dry mud. As there appeared to be more than one set of tracks, it seems possible that there was more than one creature in the woods with William and his hiking buddy that day.

Given the aggressive reaction of the Hairy One, one wonders what the hikers stumbled across that provided these intemperate actions. "William" stated emphatically that the creature struck him as intelligent but also extremely angry. Given the multiple tracks in the area, one wonders if these hikers didn't encounter a Sasquatch with a family group nearby that it felt compelled to defend.

This chasing behaviour also brings to mind another interesting cryptid creature, the Manwolf or Dogman. Many of the encounters with these dog-headed beings involve threat displays and an aggressive behaviour that seems to end once the witness is clear of a seemingly delineated area.

———

WATERTON LAKES NATIONAL PARK and its surrounds is the site of two notable Sasquatch encounters.

Thomas Steenburg, in his excellent *Sasquatch in Alberta,* documents the Crandell Lake incident extensively. This sighting is also covered in Ken Gerhard's *The Essential Guide to Bigfoot.* Steenburg does a terrific job of summarizing the sighting and then providing excerpts from his interviews with all the witnesses. His book is highly recommended to those interested in this topic.

On 23 May 1998, two couples camping at the Crandell Lake campsite in the above-mentioned park had an experience that affected them so strongly that they not only reported it to park officials but responded to an ad that Thomas Steenburg had placed in the newspaper asking for Sasquatch witnesses to come forward.

Darwin Gilles, Shannon Senkow as well as Scott and Susan Stoness were attempting to play cards that evening, but the wind was not cooperating. Finally, after the cards were blown all over the table, the two couples gave up and decided to retire for the evening. Scott and Susan followed a path to the public facilities so that they could brush their teeth.

The witnesses noted that Susan was apprehensive about being out in the wilderness after dark, so when she started at a noise in the brush, her husband simply took her hand and continued down the path to the washroom. Shortly thereafter, however, the couple encountered an animal standing on the trail in front of them. The creature grunted at them, and Susan screamed that it was a bear. She bolted back toward their camp-site, leaving her husband to follow.

As Susan ran back to rejoin Darwin and Shannon, panic appeared to set in, and the three made their way swiftly to the vehicles. Darwin and Shannon occupied one car while Susan locked herself in the other. Amusingly, Scott, when he arrived, had to get in with Darwin and Shannon since Susan would not open the door of the vehicle, even for her husband.

As this was happening, the animal that had so frightened everyone had moved off the path and into the trees. Susan was so shaken that she was worried for other campers and wanted to honk the car horn to get everyone in campsites around them out of bed. Darwin prevented her from doing this.

AFTER A FEW MOMENTS, Darwin turned on the headlamps of his car and saw nothing. He rolled down his window and shouted for Scott, in a vehicle facing the other direction, to turn on his lights. That is when they saw:

> ... an eight foot high hairy thin man-ape-like creature ... in four strides it covered the distance illuminated by the headlights, not running, just walking ... at an incredibly fast pace. Its entire body was covered with black hair. Its arms were much longer than the arms of a human. In a matter of seconds the creature had passed through the light and back into the trees, not to be seen again.

At this point, the four realized that they had seen the legendary Sasquatch. The two men wanted to get out of the cars and look for tracks, but their companions were too shocked to allow this. The women of the party simply wanted to pack up and leave. Eventually, the four compromised and took a drive around the campsite, looking for the creature.

While they did encounter one group of people who claimed to have seen "something strange", they had no further contact with the animal. After a very restless night, they reported their sighting to the park warden's office. As so often happens in these cases, the warden who came out to view the site seemed convinced that they had seen a bear. None of the witnesses would buy into this explanation. "It didn't look like a bear, it didn't walk like a bear, it didn't even resemble a bear," they stated adamantly.

Steenburg pointed out in his book that these four witnesses were all "professional, intelligent careerists" who would know what a bear looks like. Steenburg also gives little weight to the hoax theory given the size, stride, and noise of the animal. We will learn later that park officials will sometimes shoot a bear that gets too close to humans, so such a hoax would have had more than a little risk.

The second, briefer encounter occurred in 2002 when Scott Barlow, a young man training as a tour guide in Glacier National Park, took a tour bus to Waterton Lakes National Park, the site of the Crandell Lake campground. On the way back to Glacier, still in Alberta, the bus driver pointed out a "fisherman" along the side of the road. Barlow noted that the subject was "walking funny" with a "strange gate [sic]" to its stride. Further observation showed that the creature was not wearing clothes and was "hairy all over".

While Barlow supplied no further details in his report to the Bigfoot Encounters website, such as height or build of the creature, there are not a lot of candidates for this sighting. Either the witness saw a Sasquatch, or he observed a man, possibly wearing a ghillie suit. Still, given the range of observation—the witness drove right by the subject in a bus—even a person in a ghillie suit should have evidenced some footwear at that range.

Interestingly, Barlow had observed what he thought might be a Sasquatch in the mountains of Arizona when he was quite young. The Mogollon Rim area of Arizona is also known for its Sasquatch sightings, and the Hairy One has even been sighted in the desert areas of the Dinê (reservation). One of the odder things about the Hairy One is that it seems to appear wherever it pleases.

———

It seems logical to assume that people who spend more time outdoors, especially in the woods, might have a better chance of seeing a Sasquatch. That certainly seems to be the case for hunters, but, as we shall see in this incident, it may also be true for birders. This account appears on the Bigfoot Encounters website.

The witness, who identified himself as John D, his wife and their eldest son liked to watch for birds when they went to their "place in the Waskasoo area near the Red Deer River". On a summer day in 2005, the witness' wife packed a lunch for John and his son, handed them their field glasses and sent them off to see what birds they could see.

The two stopped in Canmore, on the shores of the Bow River, and were scanning the bush for various bird species when John D noticed a dark figure. "A weird feeling overcame me," the witness noted and, though he felt a bit like a Peeping Tom, he kept his glasses on the figure. He also "yelled" for his son to bring the camera, but the younger man did not respond.

John D yelled for his son again, and the figure moved a little to its right and then turned and looked toward the witness. The figure was observed against a background of trees, and John D picked out a dead tree that was slightly shorter than the figure to use as a height benchmark.

The witness, even with binoculars, was not able to make out features of the creature that he saw, but he states that it was black all over without any lines or other indications of clothing. When his son finally joined him, John D handed over the glasses and told the son where to look, but the son was unable to find the figure, and neither was the witness when he tried to re-establish visual contact.

The son suggested that his father had simply observed another birder, but when the two went down to the dead tree that John D had marked as a referent for height, they discovered that the tree was exactly nine feet tall. The figure John D had seen appeared to be slightly taller than the dead tree.

John D's son assumed that his father was mistaken about the size of the creature and that it was simply a man, but the witness was very certain of his observations. After ascertaining that there appeared to be no tracks or other sign, the two men went on to their original destination and continued to look for birds.

I am very interested in the weird feeling that overcame the witness when he sighted this being. I've noted, in other books, the idea of what ufologist Jenny Randles called the Oz Factor. In her study of UFO witnesses, one of the signs of an upcoming sighting was a feeling that something was about to happen or that something was not right. Researchers in other fields of the paranormal have noted this in their witnesses as well. While Sasquatch certainly appears as a flesh and blood creature, it is these little abnormalities that I see that keep me from lumping the Hairy One into the realm of unknown biological organism and leaving it there.

IN ANOTHER INTERESTING ENCOUNTER, taken from an interview with a witness identified as Sean on *Bigfoot Eyewitness Radio*, we have an interface between a camper and a Sasquatch that seemed to warn of its approach. Sean was a forestry worker at the time of the event and had taken some time to go camping in the Alberta Rockies near Hinton, Alberta. The man's occupation and familiarity with the wilderness adds further interest to this sighting.

The witness noted that the campsite was fifteen miles from the nearest town and that, rather than pitching a tent, he decided to sleep in the bed of his truck. He had a canopy arranged over his sleeping accommodations, and after making a campfire and drinking a few beers, he went to bed around 2100 hours. He had plans for some adventuring the next day and had decided to retire early.

At about 0300 hours, the witness awoke to the sound of

heavy footfalls. The footsteps were so heavy that they actually shook the truck, and Sean was certain that a moose or grizzly bear must be prowling nearby. He had no light, so he lay still and waited for whatever it was to pass.

Sean estimated that he had started to hear the footfalls at twenty yards out, and they continued to get closer to him and his truck. He did not see anything at that point, nor were there any unusual smells. He could hear breathing, like large lungs inhaling and exhaling. The animal seemed to sniff the truck and then walked away.

As soon as he felt it was safe, Sean decided to bug out. Whatever had approached him had come from the rear of his vehicle and then retreated in that same direction. When Sean turned his truck in a "half donut" to leave the area, his headlights fell on a Sasquatch somewhere between eight and ten feet tall.

Sean says the creature was massive with the oft-described sagittal crest, wide shoulders, and an upright, bipedal stance with "big arms swinging". The witness noted that the animal was "definitely male". The forest worker knew that he was not looking at a bear.

Additionally, Sean noted that the creature did not seem disturbed in the least by his truck or by being suddenly illuminated. It did not change its pace and did not seem in at all concerned; however, it did turn and look at him as it ambled off.

Unlike some Sasquatch witnesses, who are terrified beyond measure by their encounter, Sean stated that he did not feel the Sasquatch was threatening him and that he viewed the sighting as a positive event. At the time of the interview, he stated that he still happily camped in the woods without reservation.

Sean conjectured, in the interview, about the idea that this creature had been letting him know that it was there, alerting him to its presence with the thunderous footfalls that awakened him. I must tentatively agree with his assessment. Sasquatch witnesses often note that the creature simply seemed to appear from nowhere, that no sound heralded its approach. If the Sasquatch is capable of such ninja levels of stealth, then we might assume that this individual was letting the human know it was there.

⸺

IN ANOTHER ALBERTA Sasquatch Organization (ASO) report, #060, we find the story of a bear hunter who got more than he bargained for in a night hunt.

The witness wished to remain anonymous, but he told the ASO that he was out on a logging road, hunting bear. His wife and children were in the vehicle with him. It was about 2130 hours on a June night in 2019.

The hunter spotted what he thought was the rear end of a bear "entering the left-hand side of a cutline for a power line" as they were driving by. The man got out of the vehicle and walked down that cutline about fifty yards. As he walked up, on the right-hand side of the cutline, opposite where he had seen the supposed bear, poplar trees began to "shake violently". The hunter spied "two very large hands" parting the trees, hands with fingers the diameter of a Red Bull can. The fingers were as long as the witness' entire hand.

The witness found himself looking at what could only be a Sasquatch. He could see the forehead and nose well though the mouth was hidden by the brush. He stated that the head was the "width of a basketball, with golf ball sized eyes, a large, pronounced brow ridge, a large forehead with little hair, a flattened nose with nostrils the size of two thumbs side by side, and matted hair".

The eyes were dark brown in colour with no whites. The

witness was close enough to see eyelashes. He raised his rifle, and the creature immediately retreated into the forest, moving some distance away while the hunter's wife frantically flashed the car's lights, trying to get him to come back to the vehicle. Apparently, she had spotted the Sasquatch as well.

The witness began to move back toward the truck, and the tree shaking followed him, followed by a deep "woo" noise as he got to the vehicle. The whole group heard a loud bang on the truck roof, and the hunter sped away a short distance before pulling over to see what had hit the truck. Something had lobbed a dinner-plate-sized "clump of mud with grass in it" at the truck. The family departed the area for the evening.

This encounter is another one where a former skeptic became a believer in the reality of these creatures. When he returned to the area the next day, this witness found possible hand- and footprints as well as trees with the branches stripped away up to a height of seven feet and bark peeled down toward the ground. It should also be noted that the poplars the creature was shaking were about six to eight inches in diameter—not something that could easily be shaken by most humans.

We have seen that the Sasquatch is certainly a reality in the wilderness of Alberta. The neighbouring province of Manitoba also has a surfeit of Sasquatch cases. As with Alberta, Manitoba has different geological areas, including what is known as the Canadian Shield, the Hudson Bay Lowland, and the Interior Plains. As most of the population of Manitoba is concentrated in the southeastern corner Interior Plains region, there are large areas that could constitute suitable Sasquatch habitat, and the history of the region certainly hints at the presence of the creature in the area dating back to colonial times.

CHAPTER TWO
MANITOBA

LOREN COLEMAN, in *The Field Guide to Bigfoot, Yeti, and other Mystery Primates Worldwide*, gives us our first mystery in Manitoba. In 1784, the London *Times* reported that a group of indigenous people in the province had taken a "huge, manlike, hair-covered creature" prisoner at Lake of the Woods. After this one titillating report, nothing further appears, so we do not know if this creature was a feral human or a Sasquatch. Either way, we have no idea what disposition was made of the creature, and like the unresolved Jacko story in British Columbia, the captured creature disappears into the mists of time.

———

JOHN WARMS, in his epic book *Strange Creatures Seldom Seen*, tells the story of Paul Shabaga. For anyone interested in the strangeness Canada has to offer, I highly recommend this book, and Shabaga's story is a prime example of why I was so delighted by this text. As I read the story, I realized that the witness had also reported this encounter in BFRO report #9552 to researcher Curt Nelson under the alias Peter. Details from that report are included here as well.

Shabaga went hunting moose in November 1941. He was a young man of seventeen at the time and was seeking his prey in the Basket Creek area somewhat west of Gypsumville "with a couple of older men". There was patchy snow on the ground, and the teenager was allowed to go off on his own on this cool day. Shabaga had bad hunter's luck that day; he had fired on and wounded a moose that had then bolted off into the brush.

Tracking the animal through the snow, he spotted "a brown form behind some willows". The witness noted that, at that time, fire had not cleared out the underbrush and that it was often necessary to take one's shot through the dense willows and other undergrowth. Shabaga thought it must be the back end of his moose, so he fired on it again. The animal went down.

Shabaga indicated that he approached with extreme caution. It was not unknown for a big game animal to rally after being shot and seek to eliminate the shooter. As the witness put it: "If it wants to jump you, you have one good shot, point blank. Don't raise the gun to your shoulder, just turn it and pull the trigger. That's the last chance you got. Because a big game animal, he gets you, you've had it."

The witness' first reaction as he approached the fallen animal was "what the hell is this?" He nudged one of its feet with his boot and then turned over a hand, but it did not move. The creature was a foot and a half taller than his six feet, covered in dark brown hair and so heavy looking that Shabaga surmised that he would have had to cut willows to use as levers to turn the animal over. The bottoms of its feet and its palms were bare, and the witness stated that it was built very much like the Sasquatch in the Patterson-Gimlin film. He surmised that what he thought was the back of a moose was this animal "standing with its back to him, its neckless head bent down looking at the bloody moose track".

The teenager, after ascertaining that the creature was "stone dead", left the scene. He did not return and did not mention the incident to his hunting partners or his parents. That might seem odd behaviour for one who had just bagged one of the most sought-after animals in the world, but remember that this was 1941, well before the story of Sasquatch was well known.

One reason the witness gave for his silence was that "it was during the war years—World War II—and the thing was, people can be very funny, if you talk about something that's out of line ... right away you're crazy". In addition, the young man did not have a license for moose, so technically, his hunt was illegal. On top of all that, Shabaga was somewhat afraid of being prosecuted since there were stories in his area of feral men living as hermits in the wilderness, and he was afraid that he had accidentally shot one of these feral humans.

Shabaga had heard stories from his father of a wild man that existed in the Caucasus Mountains, but this beast did not match the image he had in his mind. Warms notes that it was thirty-five years before Shabaga realized what he had shot and longer still before he told anyone his story.

It is another of the oddities of Sasquatch lore that, even in the rare instance where someone reports shooting one of these creatures, the body is never found.

Often the shooter refuses to return to the scene of the crime. This may be due to the oft-noted idea that at least some Sasquatch have very human facial features. I can easily imagine being racked with guilt if I inadvertently shot something that looked human, and I can also see how the hunter could fear criminal consequences. After all, the body would be taken for DNA testing, and should the creature be a member of the human family tree, the legal situation could get quite sticky.

For those who do return for the body, that body is never recovered. It may simply be that the person does not have an exact location and misses the corpse. There is also a theory that Sasquatch dispose of their dead in some manner, moving the body and perhaps even burying it. Depending on the length of time before the shooter returns, it may simply be that the body has decayed and been scattered throughout the forest. As many researchers have noted, it is rare to find the body of a bear even though, presumably, bears are much more common than Sasquatch.

———

In another historical sighting, relayed to us on the *Sasquatch Canada* website from an article originally written by Laurie Mustard of the QMI Agency, Archie Motkaluk broke a fifty-year silence to tell his story. Apparently, Motkaluk had seen a TV show where a guest declared that Sasquatch did not exist, and he simply could not let the statement go since he had experienced a very close encounter with a Hairy One on 29 December 1960.

Motkaluk was home from school for the Christmas holiday and was staying with his parents on their farm near Renewer, Manitoba, southeast of Swan River. The witness had taken a horse-drawn sled three miles or so into the bush to chop firewood.

At about 1030 hours, Motkaluk was axing deadfall when he noticed a figure, about four hundred yards away, that seemed to be slowly walking in his direction. The young man thought it was another person and kept that opinion as the "person" wandered closer, stopping periodically to examine bushes.

Motkaluk wasn't sure what the other person was doing but "by the time the 'man' got within a hundred yards or so,

[Motkaluk] realized his visitor was a Sasquatch". The Hairy One went on to confront the witness at very close range, eight feet or so, and "in a manner that left [the witness] literally frozen in place till the fear subsided enough for both him and the Sasquatch to take a few steps back."

The article does not tell us how the Sasquatch went from a range of a hundred yards to very close range without Motkaluk noting its approach, but the witness' description of the animal and its behaviour fascinated the writer. According to Motkaluk, he told only his mother of the encounter when it happened, and she got him to sit down and draw what he had seen. The witness actually developed a notebook with his drawing and recollection of the event, so strongly did the sighting impact him.

Witnesses often note that a cryptid or other paranormal sighting is a life-changing event. Such an encounter often sets the witness' world view on end and leads that person to greater openness of mind regarding the strange things our world has to offer. Archie Motkaluk held his peace about his Sasquatch incident for fifty years, but the strength of the encounter was such that he had to speak out when, after all those long years, he saw media that denied the existence of the creature.

In my mind, the sheer impact of this encounter makes it stand out as a sign of the Sasquatch's presence in our world.

ON 26 JULY 1976, the Royal Canadian Mounted Police (RCMP) Norway House detachment received a peculiar report that was archived by Mary Ryan of the *Flying Saucer Review*. The chief of the Poplar River Indian Band, now Poplar River First Nation, a group of Ojibway people, told the RCMP that "many of his people" had observed a "a large hairy animal that walk[ed] on two legs".

The RCMP noted that Poplar River was about seventy-six miles south of Norway House. Officers from the detachment interviewed several witnesses, and they all stated that:

> the animal was approximately seven to eight feet tall and was very broad at the shoulders. It had the general body structure of a man only many times larger. A foot cast was taken of the foot impression that was left behind by the so-called monster and is held at this detachment. It measures 16 inches by five inches and has only three toes. Its fur is a glossy gray color, and it has white hair on its head.

The Sasquatch was powerfully built and seen swimming by one witness, but the item that stands out in the reports is a notation that the "monster" seemed "very inquisitive towards people and would come around houses on the settlement and look in doors and windows".

This curiosity about humans has been noted by so many researchers that I can't assign a specific source to it. There are multiple stories of Sasquatch peering in windows, and, in fact, we will visit the terrifying encounter of a child who experienced such an occurrence later in the book.

The question in my mind is: why? Why are Sasquatch so curious about people? Surely the elusive forest giants have had more than adequate opportunity to observe humans under a variety of conditions from the cover of their native wilderness. What is it about human beings that keeps drawing this seemingly reclusive animal out into the open when it seems that the animal is also quite shy of humans or, under certain circumstances, actively hostile to our species. My only theory in this regard is that the creature has human-level curiosity, a trait that has drawn *Homo sapiens* into many dangerous situations.

Another peculiarity of this story is the three-toed track. No known primate leaves a three-toed track, nor do they have four or six toes as described in other Sasquatch track casts. It would seem, given the sheer mass of these creatures, that a three-toed foot would be impractical, if not impossible. This is another one of those little oddities that makes us suspect there might be something more to the Sasquatch than meets the eye.

REPORTS OF SASQUATCH creatures are not rare on the ground, but the report of a professional trained observer is. Police are one of those witness groups that often draw the attention of investigators since they are not only trained to observe but must use those skills daily. Law enforcement officers tend to be reticent about reporting unusual events outside their work community, so I found the following report very interesting.

In a 1982 article in the Brantford, Ontario, *Expositor*, Constable Don Cunningham of the Dakota-Ojibway Tribal Council reported seeing an unusual creature as he and his wife, Jean, who also saw the animal, were driving from Edmonton to their home on Sandy Bay Reserve. Their three children were in the vehicle as well, but there is no note of their having seen the Sasquatch.

"The thing jumped out of the bottom of the ditch and looked at me," Cunningham stated. "At first, I thought it was a deer, until it stood up on its hind legs."

The constable described the creature as "about the size of an average man and ... covered in brown fur, although its head appeared white and it had a light grey beard". Jean Cunningham, the other witness, noted that "it had a hairy face and you could tell that it was curious ..."

Interestingly, the article notes that Cunningham actually chased the beast although it is not clear whether he did this on foot or with the vehicle. Obviously, he didn't catch it, but when he returned with friends, he found prints about forty centimetres (almost sixteen inches) in diameter that were stated to resemble a human hand. Cunningham said that "you could see the thumb mark and four fingers". The witness had noted that the creature ran like a monkey as it fled the scene. Presumably, this refers to a monkey's often quadrupedal gait.

The constable stated in the article that he planned to see if he could get the local RCMP to make a plaster cast of the print, but no follow-up article was available.

Given the below-average size of this creature and the transition from ducked down to standing up to running on all fours, one would be tempted to conjecture that this was a juvenile Sasquatch. What struck me about the article was the mention, again, of a witness having the impression that the Sasquatch was curious. It should also be noted that this is not the first time a witness had mentioned lighter-coloured hair on the head of one of these creatures. In the Ontario section that follows, we will encounter "Old Yellow Top", a Sasquatch that haunted the Cobalt area for years and was noted for its light head hair.

<hr>

WE'VE SEEN an RCMP report where local Native people said that a Sasquatch was looking in their windows and doors and a sighting from a constable and his wife that indicated the creature they saw had a curious expression. In an account from an anonymous witness, located in the *Sasquatch Chronicles* blog and entitled "Listener Shares Encounter from Manitoba Canada", we see the window-peeping behaviour again.

The encounter happened in a town called West Hawk Lake, which is located in Whitehall Provincial Park. The witness' father worked for the Department of Natural

Resources in that area, and the witness was clear that he loved the place, saying that it was a "beautiful place to be a kid". This experiencer was not afraid of the outdoors either, stating that, as he got older, he would "strike out for days at a time from our house on foot with a pack and a canoe on my back to hike and paddle the many miles of forest and lakes ..."

The observer's experience happened in April of 1984. The subject was studying hard for mid-terms, seeking to make good grades, as he had applied to join the Canadian Armed Forces in the fall, after his eighteenth birthday. Admission to the Canadian military is a fairly rigorous process and relies heavily on an extensive aptitude test as well as other screening processes, including a background investigation. The good grades that witness sought would have helped with the aptitude test and looked well for the reliability screening.

After dinner, at around 1900 hours that evening, the young man walked the eighth of a mile to a friend's house, and the two spent the evening studying.

The witness remained at his friend's house for three or four hours before taking the walk back home. In near total darkness, the prospective military member noted that he was glad for the brilliant moonlight that evening. Since there was only one streetlight in the area, a darker night would have necessitated finding his way along the road by feel. The witness arrived home, shut off the lights that had been left on for him and retired to his room. His 0500 wake-up for school would come all too soon.

The witness' room was set up with his bed on the wall. A window lay opposite the bed, and on the other side of the room was a dresser with mirror atop it. The young man looked up from getting undressed for bed at about 2300 hours and noted the "huge outline of a torso and head outlined outside my window only a few feet behind me" in the mirror.

At first, the witness thought the outline was his own reflection in the mirror, a trick of the moonlight streaming in through the window. He continued to prepare for bed but slowly realized that the supposed reflection in the mirror was not moving, even though his shadow was. He turned to look directly at the window, which was only the width of his twin bed away, and the outline was still there.

The witness' mind could not grasp what he was seeing, and he waved his arm in a slow arc. The figure outside the window did not move. Still puzzled, this experiencer crawled up onto the bed and got to within a foot or two of the window. At this point, curiosity was quickly overcome by fear as the witness realized he was looking at a figure standing on the ground and looking in his window. The witness recoiled and glanced over his shoulder, clearly seeing both himself and the creature reflected in the dresser mirror.

Moving backward on his knees, the witness fell off the bed and scuttled toward his bedroom door. Whether from the change in angle or some movement on the creature's part, the witness then saw the animal's eyes reflecting red in the moonlight.

The red eyes were the final straw. The witness raced into his parents' bedroom, waking them both, but, of course, the creature was gone when they came to see. The witness and his father stepped outside, but the ground had frozen solid, and there were no tracks. The father pointed out that the being would have to be at least eight feet tall to look in the window as indicated, and the whole incident was put off to a bad dream brought on by hours of studying.

The witness, though he returned to bed, was certain of his sighting.

I saw that thing clear as can be. It was backlit by the moon so I could make out the shape really well, besides that I was eyeball to eyeball with it. It wasn't a trick of the light, it wasn't an owl. I couldn't really make out its facial features, because it was back lit but I could see it had a wide head that came to a peak on top. It had ears like a person's sticking out on the side. Its head was like planted on its body, no neck. I could make out the jaw bone too, I could see that it was thick, like in those pictures of cave men. I didn't see the nose or mouth. When I was up against the window looking at it I didn't see the eyes either, not until I was on the other side of the room. It was the eyes that scared me. They were big, and set wide apart. They didn't look right, you know, like a deer, does when you see it in your headlights. This thing had eyes facing forward on a face that had an outline like a big man, except 4 times bigger.

The witness later took measurements at his parents' home and calculated that the animal would have been nine feet tall to fill the window frame as he remembered. While the young man continued to enjoy the out of doors, he no longer went off alone, and just recounting the story caused the hair to stand up on his arms and neck.

I always feel bad for witnesses who go to people they love for support and get the standard "you dreamed this" or "it was just a bear" or, worse yet, "stop lying" responses. If your family won't give you the benefit of the doubt after an encounter, then it makes me wonder how many Sasquatch (and other paranormal creatures and incidents) go unreported.

ANOTHER 1980s WINDOW peeper appears in a story from John Warms' *Strange Creatures Seldom Seen*. The witness, named Clifford Carriere, and a fifteen-year-old helper named Angus were trapping muskrat during the spring. The two were bunking in a cabin that belonged to Carriere's brother when the event occurred.

Carriere was awakened in the night by the sound of his dogs growling. The trapper knew that whatever had the dogs' attention was intimidating since the dog pack normally barked at intruders. The only exception that he had seen was a bear up on its hind legs. That sight had induced growling but no barking.

As the trapper listened, he heard something jostle the lid of a roasting pan out front on the top of an old refrigerator. The sound prompted the man to get out of bed, and when he heard what sounded like footsteps, he peered out the window.

Sure enough, a creature was visible—coming towards the window—but it was not a bear! Instead, it was a tall, fur-covered human-like monster on two legs—veering away as if it sensed his gaze. He watched in amazement as it ambled towards the bush —but instead of entering it, a change of mind caused it to turn and retrace its steps towards the cabin. Clifford ducked down, debating whether to go for the gun or the camera. Doing neither, he chose instead to climb back under the covers to watch what might transpire—and he was not disappointed. Momentarily, the huge figure appeared at the window, surveying the contents of the cabin for several minutes.

Carriere studied the humanlike face at his window for long minutes while trying to wake his helper so that he, too, could see the creature. Eventually, young Angus did awaken, only to find himself staring directly into the face of a monster! Fortunately for the younger man, the Sasquatch chose this time to decamp. Angus gave in to his first impulse and hid under the blankets until Carriere persuaded him that he was safe.

The two trappers left the cabin cautiously, guns in hand, to see what they could see. The roaster, which had contained the ready-to-cook muskrats, had indeed been tampered with. Its lid, which had been securely set on the roaster, was now placed off to the side. The muskrats were gone, but the creature had eaten the meat and then deposited the bones back in the roaster.

Such behaviour is atypical of predators in the wild, who will normally eat the bones of their prey. Additionally, Carriere, who had another, more long-range experience about a year later in the fall, described the fur of the creature as short and well groomed, something at odds with other descriptions Warms had of the Hairy One.

A fascinating note: Warms asked Carriere if he had been afraid of the creature, and the man responded in the negative. His people had taught him to view the creature we call Sasquatch as a protector of mankind.

This view was reinforced by a tale told to John Warms by a woman named Carrie.

———

ONE OF THE most poignant stories in *Strange Creatures Seldom Seen* is Carrie's account of her encounter with a Sasquatch.

The incident took place in the early '60s when Carrie was a girl of eleven or twelve. She lived in the remote community of Dauphin River, home to a group of Ojibway First Nations people. On a day in the late summer, Carrie was performing her usual chore of carrying water from a nearby creek to her home. It was the height of berry season, so she decided to stop and pick some cranberries.

All through the book, the reader will notice that berries and berry picking feature in a number of Sasquatch sightings. Doug Hajicek, the *MonsterQuest* producer whom we will meet later, theorized that the creatures migrate, following the ripening berries as the season for these luscious fruits progresses. It certainly seems to be the case that berries are a food source for these creatures, as we will even see a case where a Sasquatch was observed quietly eating berries.

Carrie made two mistakes in this story, mistakes that one might expect of a young person. First, she wandered away from her known routes in search of berries. Then, when she realized that she was lost, she panicked and began to run. Search and rescue experts are adamant about the need for a lost person to stay put, if possible, once they realize they are lost, but such a reaction is understandable in one so young. The outcome of the event could have been disastrous but for the timely intervention of something strange.

Carrie sprinted through the forest, hoping that she would find the edge of it and be able to make her way home. She did not find her way out of the woods, and as darkness descended and exhaustion set in, she rested on mossy hummocks. Sleep was fitful at best, as the child was worried about the animals that she knew existed in the forest, especially the numerous bears.

The young girl continued in this manner for several days, running when she could find the strength, holding her hands before her to keep branches from whipping her in the face. Even in daylight, it seemed very dark to the girl, as the forest cover was very heavy, and she cried "in desperation and fear" the entire time. She did have the presence of mind to use the berries around her for food, so she was not completely without sustenance; however, she was growing weaker with each passing day.

Night had fallen again, and the thing that Carrie feared most happened. Something large was approaching her through the forest. Certain that she was about to be attacked by a bear, the child addressed the supposed bear in her native tongue, telling it that, "I know you are going to eat me, so do it fast, and start with my head."

Carrie continued to address the unseen bear, calling it "grandfather" (a term of respect), and telling it that she was lost, that she was losing her mind with fear, that she was not large enough to fight back and that she feared she would never see her parents again. Then she waited for the inevitable.

No attack came. Whatever was in the brush moved about, stopping occasionally but not coming close. Carrie remembered that it smelled like "little puppy poop, or roots freshly dug out of the swamp". Whatever the animal was, it stayed close to her but did not approach.

The animal, whatever it was, was so close that, once she realized that it was not going to immediately eat her, Carrie reached out and touched the thing. It had long hair that reminded her of that of a beaver.

The creature did nothing but walk around, but when Carrie released her hold on its fur, the being bumped her. She almost fell and began to wonder, again, if it was simply waiting for the correct time to make her a snack.

The animal bumped her again, and they began to make progress through the wood. If the being was on her right, Carrie moved left, and when it shifted over to her left, Carrie moved right. Hours passed, and day broke. When she could see its form, the child tried to hide from the creature, but she could see it "peeking at her" through the trees, another commonly noted Sasquatch behaviour.

Carrie recognized that the creature guiding her was not a bear. It was tall and hairy and had long arms that hung at its sides like a human. The Sasquatch continued to keep her moving until she came to an area of stumps that she recognized as a place where the residents of Dauphin River had cut some trees to build an airstrip.

The girl knew where she was, and leaving the Sasquatch in the tree line, she walked out to the highway that led into her community, where she was picked up by a man and his son whom she knew.

She cried as she hugged the old man, whom she addressed as grandfather also, and told him that she had not been eaten up by a bear with long arms that looked like a monkey. The older man had laughed and replied, "Grandchild, you were blessed to be saved by the creature." He went on to say that bears don't do the kinds of things that she described. Back at home, her bruised and bloodied body told of her awful ordeal, and the pails of water that she had left behind now made perfect sense. Her parents were skeptical about her story, however, and her sisters teased her about it, calling her "the girl who touched a bear."

While her parents did not initially support Carrie's story, her father eventually told her of a very young child who disappeared into the forest only to reappear years later. When the boy learned to speak, he told the people that he had been cared for by giant monkeys. In addition, the "grandfather" who had picked Carrie up on the roadside had had an experience in which a Sasquatch supplied him with fish when he became lost.

I find it interesting to contrast these accounts with the stories of people who have had hostile interactions with Sasquatch. Why is it that the creatures seem very territorial in some cases but go out of their way to help humans in others? Like so much about this phenomenon, we just don't know, and theories about territoriality are just that, theories.

———

RETURNING TO THE JOHN WARMS' book on strange creatures, the cryptozoologist tells the story of Donovan, a young man whom he encountered at the Birdtail Sioux First Nation in 2005.

The seventeen-year-old had gone deer hunting with two younger friends near the Assiniboine River, and after fording the river, Donovan spotted several deer grazing. Suddenly, some of the deer alerted and began to run toward the hunter. Donovan stated that the deer were so spooked that they almost ran over him in their haste to flee.

Curious, the witness kept walking, and before long, he heard something moving in the bush across the river from him. "A large dark form appeared" and strode up to the river, where it embraced two trees that stood six feet apart. The creature stared at him as it pulled the two "sizeable" trees down and then released them.

Donovan watched all this through the scope of his rifle. He remembered the animal as having a "muscular build", evident in the ease with which the Sasquatch pulled down the thick trees. The being stood about ten feet tall and measured four feet or so across. The witness noted that an "awful, sewery, fishy" smell accompanied the

The young hunter seemed not to be too frightened by his encounter until the creature "put its head back and let out a powerful and fearsome scream that lasted about half a minute". At that point, Donovan's eyes began to tear uncontrollably, and he departed the area.

Splashing through icy water and swimming through deep puddles, Donovan returned to his friends, who immediately asked him why he was crying. The witness told them that he was not crying but that what he had seen made his eyes water. This statement seems to indicate that Donovan felt the creature had done something to him that made his eyes tear up. "[Donovan] pointed across the valley, and there, at the top of the far bank, stood the creature outlined against the sky".

Warms makes no note of what happened then, but if these three hunters followed the pattern of so many others, they got out of the area as quickly as they could. This extreme fear reaction in Sasquatch cases is something we will see over and over throughout the course of this book and is one that I will examine in more depth later in the text.

———

JOHN WARMS SEEMS to have spent a lot of time on First Nations reserves, and in one case, he was told that if he wanted to see a Sasquatch, he should go for a ride through Riding Mountain National Park after night fell. That is precisely what a group of young people did on 4 September 2006 at about 0030 hours.

The group was near a buffalo (bison) compound close to Jackfish Creek when they smelled a terrible odour, another frequently mentioned aspect of Sasquatch sightings. About one hundred feet from the car stood a hairy, muscular creature "with wide shoulders and a cone-shaped head". The being appeared to be breaking apart a dead tree, and as the car's occupants watched in terror, it casually flicked a "knotty little stick" toward the car. The creature then "ambled out of sight".

Some of the people in the car were afraid to take a good look at the animal, but the driver, one of two sisters in the vehicle, paid close attention. She observed:

> Green eyes reflecting in the headlights; eight-to-ten-inch-long hair hanging from long, muscular arms, coloured coffee and cream, or salt and pepper, with silver streaks; a flat, gorilla face with a flat nose and hairless brow; muscles rippling beneath the hair; legs looked like pillars, or tree stumps; no hips; almost like the creature in the movie, *Harry and the*

Hendersons—only broader; where exposed, the skin was black; fur was on the back of the hands; it could easily have thrown a log at them, but instead threw a little stick.

The other sister used words like wet dog, sewage, and fart to describe the smell of the beast.

The sisters' father took their report seriously enough to go back to the site and investigate. He retrieved the little stick that had hit the car and measured seventeen-inch footprints with a four-and-a-half-foot stride. The father also noted the dead tree, which he stated had grub tunnels in it. The deadfall was broken apart as the witnesses had said, perhaps indicating that the creature was having a snack when they disturbed it. Branches of other trees had also been snapped off higher up.

Finally, Warms tells us that the father in this incident had once hunted and killed a deer in the Duck Mountains but had failed to retrieve it after hearing an unusual, loud scream. Warms goes on to detail other hunters who have been scared out of their areas by Sasquatch sightings and vocalizations in his book *Strange Creatures Seldom Seen*.

In the *Sasquatch Chronicles* blog, we find another, very detailed story of an encounter near the Old Pinawa Dam near the town of Pinawa. The witness, who did not give her name, was in the midst of a difficult divorce and often rose early to walk, clear her head, prepare for the day, and avoid contact with her estranged spouse.

The witness was quite familiar with local wildlife. Trained as a veterinary technician, the subject had worked for the government veterinarian in the area before getting married and having children. Such work necessitated contact with both domestic and wild animals, and after she became a mother, the witness worked on a limited basis for the Department of Natural Resources doing wildlife rehabilitation.

The witness pointed out, in her written story, that Pinawa "sits right on the edge of ... wilderness. It is surrounded on three sides by Oakland [a rural municipality that has now been blended into a combined town], and the fourth side is 13km of crown land before you come to the first sparsely populated area." The town had originally been a nuclear research facility and was a planned community with lots of recreational opportunities, including a golf course and hiking trails.

In May of 2007, the witness had headed out for her early morning walk on one of these trails. The weather had improved from the frosty conditions of winter, and the snow was gone. Her description of the area is as follows:

I headed towards the dead end of the highway and across the path that was adjacent to the golf course and towards a causeway of sorts that had been created between the lake and a river channel that was a manmade diversion dam. The granite had been blasted out of the Shield and the area has many granite rock piles that have managed to acquire a few trees clinging to the sparse earth that has blown in the crevasse of those piles. So to the right of me there is the lake, to left on the causeway is a small canyon, sheer granite walls, and a drop of more than 60 feet, probably closer to 100 feet to the river below.

Oddly, the first thing that drew the witness' attention as she entered this causeway area was two crushed garter snakes, one dead and one badly twisted. The area was known to local children as a place where the snakes lived, but two things were unusual. First, the snakes of the area did not usually come out of hibernation until later in the season. Second, the snakes, which were lying clearly out in the open, should have been scavenged by the local crows.

The witness placed the live snake off to the side of the path in a grassy area and, about that time, noticed what she took to be a bear about sixty metres (two hundred feet) to her right. The animal was defecating into the lake!

The witness, wisely, scanned the shoreline for cubs but then noticed that this "bear" did not look right. As this thought formed in her mind, the creature began to stand up, and she realized that she was looking at something over eight feet tall and definitely not a bear. The being turned its whole upper body to the left, and it stood "side on" to the witness for a moment, then came out of the water "in one fluid motion".

The creature moved toward the treeline, and the witness was dumbfounded. As she put it, "the movement was like nothing I could understand ... it looked like it was on skates." She stood frozen until:

> ... it turned towards me for just a split second, showing me it's [sic] teeth and giving off a "gerrrruuufffff" sound ... that was low and rumbling. I could see its face. Not human at all ... well, I guess perhaps in some sense it was. But it was not normal at all. The eyes seemed dark, but from that distance it was more of an impression than actual sight. The mouth however was huge, it had shown me it's [sic] teeth twice, making kind of a grimacing face as it did so.

There was a "kerfuffle" in the bush about ten metres beyond the Sasquatch that she was watching, and the witness realized that there was another one of the animals in the trees. At this point, the witness decided that her only course of action was to back out of the area slowly. She began to put this plan into action, but, once again, we see the extreme fear response so may witnesses have to a Sasquatch sighting. The witness reported that her pulse was pounding in her ears and that she felt dizzy and nauseous. Her physical reaction to the sighting slowed her progress as she tried to egress the area.

Despite her debilitating fear, the witness managed to back slowly away until the Sasquatch in front of her roared while moving through the trees. She described the roar as similar to that of a lion. "It shook your insides as it blew through you."

To make matters worse, on the other side of the causeway where she was standing, the witness began to hear the telltale clatter of rocks, as though something was climbing up one of the rock piles along the trail. The subject froze once more, then began her slow backward progress again.

The witness had managed to back down the causeway past the rock pile, but, as she looked, she says that:

> I saw some movement not 20 feet from me, to the left ... and up. About 6 or 8 feet above my head and twenty feet to the left I saw the glint of auburn/brown hair. It was just an arm, a massive muscled gigantic arm was reaching around the rock pile, I could see a hand which seemed remarkably less hair covered than I would have thought, with what were clearly fingernails, thought [sic] dirt and debris covered. I distinctly remember the knuckles, which seemed very large ... like deformed large; bulbous even, almost like someone with very dire arthritic and swollen knuckle joints ... on a large hand with long fingers and attached to a ridiculously large arm.

> Two of the creatures, the black one that had roared and the other that she had spotted past the first Sasquatch, were in front of her, and a third animal seemed to be coming up the rock pile. This animal had nearly come up behind her as the other two creatures kept her attention. Fortunately, she had made enough backward progress to see the creature that seemed to be sneaking up on her, and she continued to back

out, step by step, until she came to the road, "turned tail and ran".

The witness made it about two hundred metres before being violently ill at the side of the road. She then stumbled the half a kilometre home. Within a month, the divorce was done, the subject had moved to Winnipeg and only returned to Pinawa once that summer, where she strictly avoided the bush.

As with so many witnesses, the writer of the testimony kept the story to herself for years, fearing ridicule, and only became willing to share the story when she realized how many people had seen these creatures and told their stories and that not all of them were "questionable inbred hillbillies or out and outright liars and con-artists".

This is a fascinating account, and one has to wonder what in the world these creatures were up to. There are some in the Sasquatch community that believe these animals might be responsible for some of the mysterious disappearances in the North American wilderness. This account certainly turns one's mind to such stories, but then the question is: why would a Sasquatch need or want to kidnap a human female?

A dark contemplation, indeed, and one that bears some consideration, given the many cases of Sasquatch acting out of seeming territorial aggression.

━━━

JOHN WARMS, in *Strange Creatures*, gives us another account that will put most parents on edge. He relates this tale given to him by a woman he met in the summer of 2008.

Marlene was just five years old when she went off to the fishing camp with her grandparents near God's Lake Narrows. Unlike the other times her family had made this traditional camp, this time Marlene had a new infant sister. It was Marlene's job to check on her baby sister, who lay in a hammock nearby, periodically.

Marlene was watching her grandmother "doing something with the fish" down near the shore of the lake, and it came time to go check on her sibling. The child took a path back up to the campsite, but when she reached the hammock and gazed up, she saw a "huge hairy creature" looking down at her.

Marlene remembers its long eyelashes, blinking now and then as it gazed at her, and then down at the baby, and then back at her—back and forth, its noisy breathing being the only sound it made through an open mouth that revealed big, brown-stained teeth. Its only movement was a shuffling of its feet and a slight shift of its head as it alternated its gaze, so there was nothing menacing or fearsome at all in its manner.

Because the creature did not seem actively hostile, or actively anything, for that matter, Marlene felt no fear. Instead, she felt an awe inspired by the beast's size and odd visage, and she wondered why the animal did not simply take her sister.

When the Sasquatch looked down at the baby again, Marlene bolted, running down to the lake to get her grand-mother, and she noted that the creature appeared to be turning to leave as well. The granny, of course, returned quickly, but the Sasquatch was gone.

Interestingly, in this account from a First Nations area, we see an entirely different attitude toward these creatures. Marlene's grandmother did not tell the child that she did not see anything unusual. Instead, she simply commented that "Keego-hogee [a local name for the creatures] had been there, and it had not harmed the baby."

In an amusing side note, Marlene stated that, when her grandparents later said things like "come inside now or Keego-hogee will get you", she was not afraid. She had already run into

Keegohogee, and instead of the creature being a sort of boogeyman to her, she watched for it, hoping to see it again.

We see so many instances of people, grown adults, being seized by unreasoning fear upon seeing a Sasquatch that one must wonder why this little girl felt nothing but awe in the creature's presence. Was it, perhaps, because her people accept the existence of such creatures, and, therefore, seeing the Sasquatch was no different than encountering any other wild animal? Or did the sighting, perhaps, have a deeper significance to the young girl, given her people's beliefs about the Sasquatch. This is a topic I will explore in more depth later.

⊏⊐

In their book *Beyond the Fray: Bigfoot*, Shannon LeGro and G. Michael Hopf give us an account that happened at Cedar Lake. Cross-referencing this with an interview done by Sean Forker on the *Sasquatch Encounter* podcast, I realized that the witness was Cory Lekopoy and that the event occurred in July of 2015. I'll be using both the book and notes from the interview to tell his story.

The summer had been stressful for the witness, and despite taking some time off work, his employer kept calling him. Lekopoy decided that he would take a trip from his home in Winnipeg into Northern Manitoba where his sister lived, effectively putting himself off the grid. On the long drive up north, he wanted to scout Cedar Lake and see if he could find a way in so that he, his girlfriend, and their son could come back for a camping trip later.

Lekopoy found himself on a "narrow, pothole-riddled dirt road" leading down to the lake. The road was so bad that he could travel no more than five miles per hour for fear of ripping the bottom out of his car. After coming around a turn, he could see the lake through the trees but then "caught a glimpse of something ahead of [him], about a hundred yards away". The figure was walking along the right side of the road and had its head down, "just shuffling down the side of the road".

At first, the witness felt that the figure was a person, but as he closed the distance with the walker, his perception shifted, and he began to think it was a Sasquatch. Whatever it was, it was coming close to his vehicle, but then it paused, picked up its head, "stiffened its stature and stared at [him] for what seemed like an eternity".

As we have seen in so many cases, Lekopoy was of the opinion that he could not get out of the area fast enough, but the only way for him to go was forward. The excuse for a road he was navigating was too narrow to permit a turnaround. As he puttered down toward the lake, the witness tried to convince himself that he had not seen a Sasquatch, that it had been a person as he had first thought.

When he finally arrived at the lakeshore, Lekopoy immediately turned his car around so that he could get back out. He had noted a man getting a boat into the water, so he was encouraged, assuming that the figure he had seen on the road had simply been this man's friend.

The witness got out of his car, accompanied by swarms of the horseflies ubiquitous to that area in summer, and took some pictures before making his way over to the Native fellow offloading the boat. Lekopoy asked the man why his friend wasn't helping him and got an "odd look" in return. The boater stated that he was alone, and the witness told him that he had seen someone walking up the lane. The Native man gave Lekopoy another strange look and "walked away".

Lekopoy was confused by the man's behaviour but shrugged it off, taking some more photos before returning to his vehicle. The situation was already odd, but it was about to get even stranger. Standing next to the open car door, the witness was overcome by a "feeling or sensation of dread". This type of feeling that something is going to happen is so common in the paranormal world that ufologist Jenny Randles has dubbed it one of the signs of the Oz Factor. More on this odd effect later.

Lekopoy did not get into the vehicle but instead took another photo, this time of the boater. Oddly, the man was ducking behind a Polaris Ranger as Lekopoy took his shot, and the subject soon discovered why.

> ... out of nowhere I saw something move in my peripheral view. I turned and got a good look at a massive Sasquatch. This massive creature raced in front of my car, not fifteen feet away, and into the bush.

Lekopoy hopped into his car and took off at a speed that was probably not good for the undercarriage. The vehicle was full of horseflies, so he was forced to roll the windows down to get the stinging creatures out of his car. The only thought in his mind was getting out of there and getting back to his home.

The witness noted that he was shaking uncontrollably as he made the drive away from the lake:

> To my left I heard crashing and something running on two feet. My heart was pounding, my hands were clinging to the steering wheel in a death grip, and I couldn't move fast enough. To this day, that drive to the main highway seemed to take forever. I eventually made it and headed south, as all I wanted to do was be home, in my house. What had taken me six hours to drive to in the morning I did in four hours heading back. The entire drive home I was shaking. I couldn't calm myself down. There was no doubt what I'd seen, none

whatsoever, and what made it even more terrifying was how big it was and how close it was to me.

The witness did have the presence of mind to note that he likely saw two different creatures. The first figure appeared leaner, and its colouring was dark with hair on its head and shoulders that was longer than the rest of the body hair. The Sasquatch that he saw up close seemed larger to him and was more grey in colour.

Lekopoy abandoned his plans to visit up north and instead went home to Winnipeg. He told his brother and sister what had happened, and after considerable persuasion, the brother got him to return to the site. Such was Lekopoy's residual fear that he stated that he might never have gone into the bush again if his brother had not persuaded him to revisit the scene of his sighting.

While one might not be surprised to know that Sasquatch inhabits the wilderness of Manitoba, it may come as a surprise to some that the forest giants are also often seen in the most populous province of Canada: Ontario.

CHAPTER THREE
ONTARIO

ONE SASQUATCH CASE in Ontario was interesting enough to catch the attention of both Loren Coleman, in his *The Field Guide to Bigfoot, Yeti, and Other Mystery Primates Worldwide,* and Ken Gerhard, in his *The Essential Guide to Bigfoot.* Dubbed Yellow Top or Old Yellow Top, this creature was sighted in the area of Cobalt, Ontario, possibly as early as 1906 and was last seen in 1970. If the creature described was the same one in all instances, then, as Gerhard points out, these sightings indicate that Sasquatch may live to sixty years or more.

The incidents around Cobalt began in September of 1906 when workers reported seeing "an odd, upright figure lurking just near the edge of the timberline". In late July 1923, two prospectors, Lorne Wilson and J. A. MacAuley, came across a large critter eating blueberries from a bush. [Author's note: Blueberries will play a key role in another set of sightings related later in this section]. Of course, the two men assumed they were looking at a bear until Wilson threw a stone at the blueberry-eater. To the men's astonishment, the animal stood up and walked away on two legs.

The two prospectors were able to determine that they were not looking at anything ursine but instead described a being covered in black fur. Further, they stated that the creature had longer hair on its head that appeared to be blonde or golden, thus the Yellow Top moniker.

In April 1946, over twenty years later, a woman and her child, who were walking the railroad tracks into Cobalt, observed a being that "walked almost like a man". The woman described the creature as a dark, hairy animal with a "light head". It walked off into the bush, seemingly headed toward Gillies Lake.

Old Yellow Top, or a similar-looking offspring, made another dramatic appearance in August of 1970. The creature crossed the road in front of a bus carrying twenty-seven miners to their night-shift jobs at the Cobalt Lode, a mine containing cobalt, silver, copper, and other minerals. The appearance of the animal so startled the bus driver, Aimee Latreille, that he lost control of the vehicle and nearly plunged into a nearby rock cut.

Latreille stated that he thought he was looking at a giant bear until it turned and looked into his headlights. The driver could see the light hair, down to the shoulders. He had heard of the creature from local lore but became certain of its existence after the incident. One of the miners at the front of the bus, Larry Cormack, also spotted the creature and said that it looked like a bear "but it didn't walk like one. It was kind of half stooped over".

1906 to 1970 is a span of sixty-four years. While it is possible that Sasquatch live this long, it had also been noted that these creatures appear in what look like family groups from time to time. Unless the local Sasquatch have taken up hair dying as a hobby, it seems likely that the same creature was being seen over the decades in the Cobalt area or that the blonde mane was a genetic trait passed on to other animals born into the group. I've not found any other reports of this light-topped Sasquatch after the bus incident, but this tiny town along the Ontario-Quebec border is far from the only place in Ontario where Sasquatch have been seen.

———

WE'VE SEEN that Old Yellow Top seemed to be frequenting the forests of Northern Ontario from the early 1900s to 1970, but another fascinating story from the Bigfoot Encounters website occurred in 1968. The witness, Edward Scott, was seven years old at the time of his sighting and had not spoken of the incident to anyone but his mother until he wrote it down in 2012.

We see this sort of behaviour in witnesses to the strange all the time. I've often wondered, if we removed the fear of ridicule from the witness equation, how many people would come forward to tell their experiences of unexplained events.

The witness lived in the tiny town of Terrace Bay in the northwestern portion of Ontario. The first odd thing to happen, in Scott's recollection, was that that town put a curfew into place so that all children had to be indoors before it was fully dark. Scott's father told the boy that the curfew was needed to protect against "the Boogeyman", a creature that would hunt the night for disobedient children who were not in their beds by 2100 hours each night.

Scott's parents also took the occasion of a bear raiding their trash, while the child watched out the back door, to drive home the point that it was not safe for children to be out anywhere near nightfall. One has the impression, in reading the witness' story, that the parents were using the Boogeyman and bears to be certain their little ones did not venture out into the darkness.

The boy discovered yet another reason not to disobey the rules in early August of that year. Scott shared a room with an older brother, and the brother had fallen asleep with the light on. The seven-year-old, unable to wake his brother, got out of bed to turn off the lamp, which was keeping him awake. As he came close to the night table where the lamp sat, he saw:

> ... The silhouette of a tall, somewhat hunched back, long hairy armed prowler with an ape like profile moving toward the gate of our backyard. As it was passing by my window, my hand trembled as I reached to open the clear-white curtain just a little so I could see the figure [*sic*] whole face. I moved the curtain. It stopped and turned to face the window. Terrified, I quickly turned off the light ... ran to my bed, jumped in and threw the covers over my head.

As a side note, this behaviour of throwing the covers over one's head seems to be a universal "hide from the face of the strange and/or frightening" gesture. While the behaviour is most often seen in children, we also read about it in adults faced with something they can't understand. One wonders if throwing the blankets over one's head is not a fear-induced regression to that time in human development when the child believes that, if they cannot be seen, then they will not be noticed.

Since, at that time, Sasquatch was virtually unknown in the wilds of Canada, Scott assumed that he had seen the threatened Boogeyman. Interestingly, in the morning, the boy's mother discovered that her garden had been trampled. The father conjectured that the damage was the result of a moose or large bear and took a hunting party of men into the woodland at the bottom of a steep hill with no results.

Scott told his mother about the sighting but was told, in no uncertain terms, not to speak of such things. As I noted above, he took this advice to heart and did not reveal his sighting for forty-four years.

———

JOURNALIST BILL STEER, writing on the *Sootoday.com* website, quotes a story told to him by pre-eminent Sasquatch researcher Dr. John Bindernagel. This story, which occurred in 1982, is fascinating since the witness had not one but two up-close encounters with a Sasquatch, one right after the other.

William (Bill) Webster was a retired dairy farmer moose hunting near Wildgoose Lake in Northern Ontario. He had just used a moose call when he received an unexpected response: "a 'club' being swung downwards by a large animal hidden in the adjacent bushes".

Webster was certain that, if the good-sized limb had hit him, he would not have been around to make his report to the well-known Sasquatch researcher. The witness could see some black hair through the bush, but the hair was higher than his head. He took the safety off his rifle and pointed it toward the general area of the chest in case he was required to shoot.

Whatever was in the bush retreated silently, but Webster then counted five rocks thrown at him and decided to vacate the area before he was struck by one. He was walking along a logging road and, as the day was getting warmer, reached up to unbutton his shirt. To his shock, a Sasquatch stepped out of the forest directly in front of him.

The creature was walking away from Webster. The hunter described having his rifle scope sighting onto the animal's spine and said that it was "seven or eight feet tall" with short legs and long arms. The arms fell from wide shoulders well down its legs, and the creature remained on two legs for the entire time of the sighting.

Webster stated that the animal moved slowly, "as if it wasn't in a hurry". The Sasquatch was dark-haired but not black, and the hair was not long, perhaps one or two inches. As is so often described, the creature had a rounded head, and the "sides of the neck went straight up to the head".

As noted, Webster had good aim on the creature but later stated that it "had more right to be here [the woodland] than I did". He did not take the shot but did later backtrack the animal from where it had come out of the brush. He found big foot-prints of at least a foot in length with five toes "like a human". He stated that the toes were "square across" not slanted toward the small toes like a human track. The foot made an imprint even on dry ground.

The story is interesting for several reasons.

First, the use of a club and then thrown stones to scare off the hunter gives us an indication that, where such things are directly observed, they point to a tool-using being. Bears do not try to frighten people with clubs, throw stones at them or walk bipedally for any distance.

Second, please note the hunter's reaction to having a Sasquatch in his rifle sights. Webster did not even consider shooting the creature and further stated that he felt that the Sasquatch had more right to be in the forest than he did.

I can't help but think of the indigenous belief in these creatures as guardians of the forest. Note that in the story of Paul Shabaga, earlier in the book, his shooting of a Sasquatch was done quite by accident. I don't ever remember encountering the story of someone claiming to shoot one of these animals once they identified what it was.

In later sections of the book, we will encounter Sasquatch that speak to people mind to mind, so perhaps this failure to shoot is a result of a kind of telepathic influence. Perhaps Webster's feeling that the Hairy One had more right to be in the forest than he did was an example of mind control. Or it may simply be that people looking through the scope of a rifle at a Sasquatch note just how much these creatures look like people. At least one hunter has said that they couldn't pull the trigger on a Sasquatch because they felt that doing so would be murder.

Our next report is the continuation of one that we cited in the Alberta section and is notable because of the quality of the witness.

IN THE ALBERTA section of the book, we looked at a sighting from a Special Forces soldier out doing maintenance work for his brigade during a training mission. This individual, who tells his story on the *Alberta Sasquatch Organization* website (incident #066), also had an earlier encounter with something unknown, this time in the forests of Northern Ontario. While this was not a visual sighting, I felt the need to include it for completeness' sake.

The soldier was based in Petawawa with the Special Operations Force, which is known today as the Joint Task Force or JTF. This event occurred the winter before his May 1983 visual sighting. The witness' group was out on a winter survival training course approximately two to three kilometres from Algonquin Provincial Park, a massive wilderness area about three to four hours north of Toronto.

During the day, the team was busy doing training exercises, but at night, things calmed down, and the only activity, other than sleeping, was guard duty. During one of these training nights, the witness was awakened for his guard shift. The weather conditions were less than optimal, with a temperature of -30 Celsius (-22 Fahrenheit), and "the wind was blowing like crazy".

The mission was simple: keep an eye on the three tents housing people and the single tents that held their supplies. Basically, the duty was a fire watch designed to be sure that personnel and supplies were kept safe. The soldier noted that they were in bear country and that there were plenty of other animals in the area: "fishers, wolf, coyote ... the whole deal".

The witness was walking his tour when he heard "some talking down the mountain" just inside the tree line off a rocky protuberance about a third of the way down the slope. He first heard a voice speaking and then a reply from a location one hundred and fifty to two hundred metres away. "The voices sounded Japanese, like in the samurai movies ... pretty much the same".

Such statements, of course, recall the famed samurai chatter from the so-called Sierra Sounds.

The soldier was puzzled. It was extremely dark, and the only light source was a lantern lit back at the campsite. He tried to use his own flashlight to penetrate the gloom but still could see nothing. He decided to try to make contact with the owner of the voices and announced his presence, advising the speakers that they were on a military base and needed to identify themselves. The witness had a rifle with him, but no bullets had been issued for the training exercise.

The soldier tried to contact the source of the voices for over half an hour but eventually got frustrated. While he had no bullets, he did have a bayonet, and he affixed this to his rifle, determined to root out the troublemakers. Even with this weapon and his aggressive announcement that the speakers needed to identify themselves, no one came forward, and eventually the voices stopped.

His guard tour was nearly up, so the witness returned to camp and woke his replacement. As he put it, "I didn't tell him a thing. Otherwise, he would have thought I was crazy and that something was wrong with me."

The witness was clear in his report that he had no real way to determine what was speaking on the side of that mountain. All he could say about the event was that the sounds were not the normal animal sounds that he was familiar with. He stated that he was at home in the woods, having been a hunter since he was young, and that he had never heard anything like the voices in the woods previous to his encounter.

The skeptic might wonder if he didn't encounter some people up on that mountainside, but I find this hard to credit. The temperature was sub-zero, and there was a wind chill. My area of Canada is a little more temperate, but I can testify to the sheer drilling force of a winter wind in this area. One does not want to be out in that sort of weather unless it can't be avoided.

Additionally, it was pitch dark. Why would anyone in their right mind be out on a mountainside in the dark in that above-mentioned weather? Even if we did have a group of hoaxers, dressed for the conditions, with night-vision equipment to see their way, why would they choose to harass a group of armed soldiers? Such a supposition strains credibility.

And then there is the matter of the chatter itself. If this theoretical group of hoaxers actually did manage to carry out their prank, why speak in a "language" that sounded like Japanese? Why not French or even pig Latin? It seems clear to me that there was something unusual on that mountainside with the soldier. I will discuss these nonvisual encounters in a later section of the book.

⊏⊐

FROM SPECIAL FORCES soldiers to police officers, civilians are not the only people who see Sasquatch. In a brief report to the

Bigfoot Field Researchers Organization (BFRO #10611), a Durham regional police officer and hunter since childhood reported a sighting in Northern Ontario about one hundred miles west of Cochrane. The report is slightly edited for spelling.

> I was going moose hunting and my friend was driving. We had been on the road about 9 to 10 hours going to Igness Ontario. We were about 100 miles west of Cochrane Ontario on the Trans-Canada hwy. This area has the bush cut back some 30 to 40 yards on each side of the road when I noticed an animal coming out of the north side of a ditch area and run across a two lane hwy. We were about 100 yards away and moving up fast as we were driving at about 65 to 70 mph (100 to 115 klms). This animal ran across the road on two legs and were about 20 yards away. By the time it crossed the road my friend turned to me and said, "What the hell was that?" I said don't you know that was a Sasquatch/a Bigfoot. He turned to me and said it was not. I'm not going to have people call me nuts, so I said, OK? What was it? He said a man in a fur suit.

Again, we see the fear of ridicule raise its ugly head. The two men argued about what they had seen for a few minutes before, apparently, agreeing to disagree. The officer notes that his friend still would not speak of the incident at the time of the report.

The witness further reported that the episode happened in the evening between 1900 and 2100 hours. The creature was described as six to seven feet tall with arms that hung down to its knees and fur that reminded the witness of moose pelt. The animal crossed the two-lane highway in five or six steps and then continued into a roadside ditch.

An investigator contacted the witness (no name listed) and

got some additional details. The Sasquatch appeared to be female, as the witness could see breasts. The officer guessed the creature's weight at approximately three to four hundred pounds with heavy legs and buttocks. He testified that he could see the play of muscles in the animal's shoulders as it crossed the road and that it turned its torso to look at the truck as he and his companion watched.

The witness also noted that he had a camera in the vehicle but that he was so shocked at what he was seeing that it did not occur to him to try to take a picture.

I often hear people wonder why, in this age where almost everyone has a camera with them, no one has gotten a good clear picture of a Sasquatch. So-called skeptics love to trumpet this one, but my rebuttal to this is simple—any person, coming suddenly on a large, presumably wild animal, is going to have a moment's hesitation.

Suddenly coming into proximity with such a large creature causes responses that I suspect are programmed into the most ancient parts of our brains. Now, add to this initial shock factor the idea that the creature you are looking at is not supposed to exist. I can easily see how someone's brain might be scrambled in such a situation, and the idea of a camera would go flying straight out of their head.

This reaction could account for all the blurry photos that are shot of the creature as well. Even if one can overcome the shock reaction and get the camera out, adrenaline will be flowing, and the hands will, as a result, be shaking. It's hard enough to take a good picture when one is calm and able to take one's time. Photography becomes exponentially harder when one is shaking and the subject is, often, moving.

WE MOVE from a Durham regional police officer to counsellors at a scout camp near Lake Christie, Ontario, for our next sighting. The witness, who identified himself as J on the Bigfoot Encounters website, had a visual sighting in 1998 during the course of his employment at the camp and mentioned a couple of other events during the time he worked there (1996–1998).

The visual sighting occurred in August of 1998. The summer was winding down, and the younger campers had left for the season, so J had decided to sleep with a group of counsellors over in the "Cub Field" on the evening of the event. The field was a large clear space, about one hundred fifty yards wide and two hundred fifty yards long with a row of cabins on either side. The whole clearing stood in the midst of dense forest.

J had bunked down in one of the cabins but found himself inexplicably awake around midnight. The witness thought that there was howling in the distance but didn't think that this would awaken him, as he was used to wilderness sounds at night. J checked to see if a cabin mate was awake, and the other counsellor was dead asleep.

J described the event as follows:

> Then, out of nowhere, I heard what I thought was someone running right by my cabin. The steps were heavy and quick. I shot out of bed, grabbing my flashlight, wondering who was running around at this hour, since everyone was supposed to be in bed hours ago. I swung the door of the cabin open and shone my flashlight in the field. I couldn't believe what I saw next.
>
> About 40 feet, diagonally from me, I saw a large, hairy creature walking across the field, very swiftly. I stood there in shock, wondering what my eyes were seeing. This thing was absolutely enormous! At first I thought it might be a bear, but then I realized something—it was walking upright, on two

legs. It was very tall, bulky and had dark brown hair covering its entire body.

The creature seemed to notice J's flashlight and turned to look at him. J described the face as "ape-like having little hair" and noted that the eyes reflected yellow. The skin on the face was almost the same dark colour as the hair. The two stood looking at each other for a few seconds, during which time J noticed an odour so foul that he was forced to plug his nose to avoid vomiting.

The being continued on its way, disappearing into the forest. J looked for tracks the next day and found nothing but did estimate, based on his own height of six feet, that the animal was at least eight feet tall.

As often happens with witnesses to a Sasquatch (and other highly strange events), J suffered from recurring nightmares and sleepless nights after the incident. Amazingly, J returned the following summer, thinking that the incident was a once-in-a-lifetime occurrence, and experienced a rock-throwing event while rowing with a romantic interest in the lake. He might have put this off to camp pranksters if he had not again encountered yellow eye reflection when he and the young lady shone flashlights on the shore. Additionally, during the summer of 1996, J reported hearing howling near the camp that he was unable to identify.

Witness Curt Beleutz, writing on the Bigfoot Encounters website, gives us another sighting from the Algonquin Provincial Park area. As the reader will recall, the Canadian Forces soldier had his chatter encounter in this area, and we will see other sightings near this large area of wilderness.

Beleutz and a group of friends were camping in the far North Bay region of the park. It is important to understand that this park is 7,653 square kilometres, so it covers a considerable amount of area in Ontario, with much of that area not accessible to motor vehicles. Beleutz and his friends were actually in one of the developed areas of the park, and their truck was parked nearby.

At about 0045 hours, the campers had seated themselves next to a campfire. The witness stated that the "moon was pretty bright", and they also had light from a campfire, so the visibility in the area was good. As they sat next to the fire, the area was permeated with a "odd smell" that Beleutz likened to "a wet dog and rotting meat".

There was a sound near the friends' truck, and they went to investigate, thinking they might find a raccoon or bear.

> We saw a creature that looked like a bear, crouched down near the truck, probably watching us. We yelled at it, thinking that this bear would run away. But it did not. It stood up and stared at us from a distance of about ten feet from us. This is when we saw that this was not a bear. We continued to yell at it, not knowing what the hell it was. It stared at us while we yelled at it until I guess it got annoyed and yelled right back.

The witness describes the sound the creature made as "ear piercing and deep". The sound seems to have produced the typical fear reaction in the group. Beleutz pointed out that the creature was much bigger and wider than his six-foot, two-inch frame.

Almost as soon as the creature vocalized, a gunshot sounded, and the Sasquatch ran off into the woods. A ranger had been checking campfires in the area to make certain they stayed in control, and when the group told their story, he dismissed the sighting as a bear.

Beleutz and his friends were so certain they had not seen a bear that they packed up and left as the ranger watched. They described the creature as too big to be a bear, standing on two legs and with a face that they emphasized was human appearing with a flat nose (unlike the snout of a bear).

The creature also had "cow-like molars" that the group saw when it opened its mouth to "yell" as well as "big black eyes" that looked out from a leather-skinned face. Finally, Beleutz and his friends noted that the animal was covered in hair about six inches in length and, as noted earlier, smelled foul.

I find it interesting that the warden's first reaction, upon hearing the campers yelling and seeing something in their camp-site, was to fire a shot. Algonquin is populated by black bears, not the more aggressive grizzly. Black bears are so shy that Dr. Lynn Rogers, in an article for the North American Bear Center website, states that he has not even been attacked by mother bears while trying to remove cubs from a den.

So why would the warden's first reaction have been to fire a shot? That would certainly scare the bear away but so, too, should the shouts of the onlookers. I would not be surprised if the warden knew exactly what he or she was looking at and had some experience driving the creatures away. As I said at the beginning of the section, Sasquatch reports are rife in this area.

━━━

HUNTERS ARE people who spend a great deal of time outdoors and, in my opinion, make excellent witnesses. They are not easily spooked by sounds or movement in the forest, and safety classes teach them to verify their targets before they shoot. No one wants to make a mistake like the one young

Paul Shabaga made and shoot something they did not intend to shoot.

When the witness is a fifty-year-old hunter who began shooting when they were seven years old, started hunting deer at about fourteen or fifteen and had been hunting moose fourteen or fifteen years prior to the incident, we have to sit up and take notice. When that hunter also turns out to be a Toronto police veteran of twenty-eight years, one expects that the investigators with the Bigfoot Field Researchers Organization (BFRO) were in spasms of delight.

The witness, who had to remain anonymous considering his occupation, was moose hunting in the area of Searchmount, some thirty miles northeast of Sault Ste. Marie, and had an encounter. This sighting might have been lost to the fear of derision if the witness had not related it to his wife via telephone. She talked to a co-worker and discovered the BFRO website. She let her husband know that there were a number of Ontario sightings in the BFRO database, and this helped convince the poor man that he was not "losing [his] marbles".

Police officers write reports—lots of reports—and this officer made careful note of times as he recorded the episode. The date was 14 October 2003, and the witness had ridden an ATV up a dead-end trail. He got stuck in the mud but managed to get the ATV unstuck, then headed back down the trail until he came to a clearing where he set up to hunt, establishing a clear field of fire, spreading moose cow urine, and sounding moose calls.

The clearing was about two hundred yards long, north to south, and the witness stopped there about 0745 hours. He had completed his preparations by 0805 and started to settle in to wait when it began to rain at about 0815. He didn't want to get his firearm wet, so he stored it in the gun boot on his ATV.

The witness noted that, while the rain helped to wash away his scent, it made the woods noisy, with the falling rain obscuring a lot of sounds. At 0830, however, he began hearing "footsteps and snapping twigs" to the northeast of his position. The consistent patter of the rain disguised the movement sounds until they were quite close to the witness. Suddenly, he heard the distinctive sound of a bull moose "raking his rack on the brush". Moments later, the moose appeared from the forest about seventy yards from where he sat.

Reaching for his weapon, the hunter accidentally dropped the gun cover over the tank of the ATV, making a banging noise. The moose promptly disappeared into the bush. The witness found this behaviour odd since his experience of moose was that they were not afraid of anything. He stated that he had seen moose stand and stare at him, unconcerned, on several occasions. Though he tried to attract the moose's attention with calls, the bull was gone.

The witness called his brother-in-law on the radio, and the two determined exactly where the moose had exited the brush. The hunter decided to set up about five yards from where he had seen the bull in hopes of it returning. He repeated his preparations, spraying urine and making some calls, then settled in to wait.

It was about 1230 hours when he took his position, deciding that he would wait on the moose until the end of the hunting day. He lunched, stretched his legs, had a few smokes, and even took a short nap. The hunter and his brother-in-law had found that the moose had slipped away in a gorge, which was now behind the witness.

At 1330, he began to hear heavy thumps behind him, on an intermittent basis. The thumps sounded like "a stone or something heavy hitting the ground", but the witness was unable to see anything when he turned to look. He noted specifically that the thumps were louder than the still falling rain.

At 1725 hours, the officer had dismounted the ATV to have

a cigarette and placed his weapon in the gun boot at the front of the vehicle. Once more he heard the noise of footsteps, crunching leaves and snapping twigs, coming from the gorge behind him. Thinking that the moose had finally returned, he retrieved his firearm and gazed into the gulley.

At a range of about forty yards, he saw what he at first took to be a man walking in his direction. The subject appeared to be having some difficulty navigating the terrain and grabbed a tree to swing itself around and duck behind some thick cover. The figure seemed to be dressed all in black with a black tuque or balaclava on his head. The impression of a cap was reached because the officer noted that the subject's head "seemed to be long at the back like a man wearing a tuque". It also appeared to the hunter that the figure was wearing a jacket that was open halfway to reveal a different-coloured inner liner, "light gray or almost blue on the chest area in the shape of a V".

As he continued to observe the figure, the officer became more and more convinced he was not seeing a human:

> I couldn't really say how tall it was because his legs were behind thick brush and I could only see to about mid thigh. But I would have guessed at the time that he was anywhere from 5'8" to 6' tall. But he was about 40 yards away and it's hard to judge height or size in the bush when you're not sure of the distance. His arms seemed too long for a man but he was extremely muscular, like a body builder with the typical "V" shape build. There was definitely no fat on him at all. I could see the different muscle groups on his upper body and arms bulging out and could see that it had a washboard stomach. When he grabbed the tree I saw that he had hands, not paws. He swung around the tree and dove for cover as if trying to hide from me. As I said earlier, it was a dull day and

was raining and he looked wet. He was covered with black or dark brown hair and it looked like the hair was stuck to him fairly closely because he was wet. What also gave me the body builder impression was that he seemed to have no neck, or he had so much muscle on his shoulders that it gave that appearance. On top of all this his shoulders were extremely broad.

After the creature disappeared into the brush, the hunter heard "a hoarse, raspy cough" as well as a howl that sounded like that of a wolf, only much deeper.

After coming to the realization that he had likely seen a Sasquatch, the officer decided that, though he never left a hunting site until it was full dark, he was going to come out early that day. His intention was to return the next day and look for the bull moose he had seen, but he "couldn't bring [himself] to go back to that area the next day". The officer noted that it was the first time in thirty-five years that he had been afraid in the bush.

The witness decided to hunt different areas to finish out his hunt and did not get a moose during that trip. The BFRO field investigator wondered, along with the witness, if the Sasquatch hadn't scared the bull moose seen earlier in the day away. The person from BFRO who followed up also noted that the officer was in the skeptic camp until he had his own sighting. It is a measure of the impression that the Sasquatch makes on witnesses that they are so certain of what they have seen that they abandon previously skeptical positions immediately on seeing the creature. Witnesses know what they have seen, even if others don't believe them, and as we have seen, the sighting stays with them over decades.

This report, with its date and time notations and the very detailed description of a Sasquatch in the wild, is an investigator's dream. In the next section we will look at a sighting from another terrific witness, a forestry worker.

———

I BELIEVE witnesses unless I have good reason not to, but even I will admit that some witnesses instantly have more agency than others because they are trained observers. I've already given the report of a Canadian Forces special operator and a Toronto police officer in this section.

In a BFRO report (#23171), we get the testimony of a forestry worker, a person who, by the very nature of their business, spends extended amounts of time in the woods and knows the woodland intimately. This episode occurred about sixty-five kilometres from Matheson, Ontario, in September 2006.

The witness and his partner were "obtaining information to determine the health of the forest" in a plot about seven hundred metres off the road where they had parked their truck. The two measured the trees in the plot they were working and had begun to determine the age of some trees in the plot when they heard a sound like "an old rotten log being ripped apart just metres from where [they] were working".

Thinking that there was a bear in the area, the witness retrieved a can of bear spray as well as a tool he needed for his work from his nearby vest. When he returned, his partner advised that the animal in the woods had circled around them in the general direction of their vehicle. They could hear heavy footsteps and thought that the bear was likely avoiding them.

The two workers continued to work and had just taken a soil sample when a piece of rotten tree root "was thrown into the canopy above us, crashed past branches, arched over toward us and landed just to the left of where [the witness] was standing". The witness' partner jumped to his feet, pronouncing the incident "f***ing weird", and then the two discussed whether any other workers might be in the area. Perhaps the incident was a prank?

After another, smaller stick landed near them, the witness became angry and walked in the direction from which the objects were coming. The witness spotted something in the forest and related the following:

> I'm standing absolutely still thinking to myself, who would place an 8ft tall haystack here in the middle of nowhere? It was a precarious-looking haystack. Then I realize it's not a haystack. I remember thinking to look away before you scare it or it moves. My heart and breathing lost rhythm, and shock prevented me from moving normally. I caught my breath painfully enough so I could walk back to my partner. Decisions and memory felt distorted and everything raced through my mind as I continued toward my partner. I asked myself over and over, did that just happen? DID THAT JUST HAPPEN? When I arrived back to the work site about 200–300 metres away, my partner asked. "So, what is it?" I replied "Nothing, let's finish up quick, and get the f@#k out of here." I never told poor Luke who continues working out there what I saw that day, or that I was treated for anxiety as a result when we returned home.

BFRO investigator Todd Prescott clarified the sighting with the witness, finding that the creature was standing with its back to the witness with its head forward, seemingly looking at the ground. The being was six to eight feet tall but estimated at six hundred pounds with a broad-shouldered, square look to it and long, flowing hair of a light brown or yellowish colour. The creature's arms were long and held still at its sides.

The being stood perfectly still as the witness observed it for a period of about five seconds. There was no sound or odour detected around the creature, but Prescott noted that the witness was subject to anxiety attacks in the time that followed this sighting. We will see, in a later incident in this section, another traumatic episode that resulted in the "nervous break-down" of the witness.

———

OTHER THAN SIGHTINGS IN BC, perhaps one of the best-known Canadian Sasquatch events occurred at Snelgrove Lake in Ontario, a site in the north of the province so remote that one must fly in to visit it. I am using a combination of information from the TV show *Monster Quest* and a *Sasquatch Chronicles* interview with the show's producer Doug Hajicek. I've derived some additional background information from Preston Dennett's book *Bigfoot, Yeti, and Other Ape-Men*.

Doug Hajicek grew up in the woods and had his first taste of the mysterious while filming a nature documentary in the subarctic. He had been filming giant lake trout and went to shore for a call of nature where he discovered a track line running through pea gravel into the "stunted" black spruce forest. The tracks were not super detailed, but they seemed to lack the telltale claw mark of a bear, and the track line was perfectly straight.

Hajicek asked one of the large members of his party to jump off a rock in an effort to duplicate the tracks, and the individual "couldn't even make a dent". Whatever made the tracks was very heavy and showed evidence of stepping over trees. The producer realized that he might be following the trail of a Sasquatch and endeavoured to get the float plane pilot into the air to try to track the creature down. The pilot, sure he was being hoaxed, flatly refused.

80

After this experience, Hajicek, like so many witnesses before him, became obsessed with getting answers and stated that he used Sasquatch documentaries as a way of gathering information on the creature while still earning a living. This brings us to the set of *MonsterQuest* episodes that document the ongoing Sasquatch incursion at Snelgrove Lake. Hajicek says that he has seen Sasquatch on three occasions, including a visual encounter at the lake.

TV must market itself, and fear sells, so the titles of these two episodes—"Sasquatch Attacks" and "Sasquatch Attacks II" —are, perhaps, a bit melodramatic, but it does seem that people staying at this remote cabin have had experiences that indicate that something is trying to get them to leave. While the camera crews and scientists did not capture footage of Sasquatch, this is a case with some physical evidence as well as lots of Class B type phenomenon.

Early in the first *MonsterQuest* episode, we learn that the cabin was ransacked sometime before the TV crew came to investigate. *MonsterQuest* brought in an expert on bears, Dr. Lynn Rogers, a wildlife biologist who specializes in bears. He viewed video of the cabin taken for insurance purposes and opined that the damage was not done by a bear. Rogers based his finding on the fact that there did not appear to be claw and/or teeth marks in places where he would expect to see them.

The wildlife biologist was especially interested in the refrigerator, which was turned over. Apparently, in bear incursions on a cabin, the refrigerator is frequently mauled since the insulation contains formaldehyde, which smells to a bear like the formic acid associated with ants. Refrigerators are thus usually subjected to much abuse as the bear attempts to get the non-existent ants. The telltale tooth and claw marks were not present in this cabin invasion.

Rogers also performed morphological examination of hair found at the site. He found that the hair was definitely not from a bear and, after comparing it to other North American species, concluded that it most resembled human hair. There was, however, no medulla, as there would be with human hair, and the tip of the hair was naturally worn and had never been cut.

After the trashing of the cabin, its owner, Chuck Mosbeck, placed a board with screws driven through it in front of the door. These boards are used to deter bears since, as you might imagine, stepping on one is painful. In this case, however, something that did not appear to be a bear stepped on the board.

The board was a source of great interest to the team that flew into the cabin with the *MonsterQuest* crew. Dr. Jeff Meldrum, the anthropologist from University of Idaho who specializes in Sasquatch track casts, and Dr. Curt Nelson, a biologist from the University of Minnesota, got blood and tissue samples from the bear-deterrent board.

Additionally, on the show, they played a game of connect-the-dots with areas where tissue and blood had been found on the board and came up with an outline that looked like a Sasquatch print. After some setbacks, the *MonsterQuest* team was able to get a DNA analysis from the blood and tissue, which, in the first show, concluded that they were dealing with primate DNA, almost identical to human DNA, with only one distinctive difference.

Despite trying wood knocking to elicit a response from the local Sasquatch, claiming that this is a common communication method amongst primates, there seemed to be no reaction to team's presence until the last night of the investigation. A member of the film crew, not wanting to go off to the outhouse in the dark, urinated off the front porch. Almost immediately, a rock was thrown from the bush, narrowly missing the crew member.

Curt Nelson picked up a rock and lobbed it back into the forest. A rock then sailed up over the cabin and landed on the tin roof. The film crew and the scientists retreated into the house, and there seemed to have been an abnormal fear reaction to the event. Oddly, one poor cameraman was left outside to scan the tree line with thermal and night-vision equipment, to no effect.

The *MonsterQuest* team was picked up in the morning, but before they left, the surrounding woodland was searched, and no evidence of the intruders that were hurling stones the night before was found.

MonsterQuest returned to the Snelgrove Lake cabin in an episode in their second season, and this episode overlaps with a sighting some distance from the lake cabin.

———

IN THE SECOND "SASQUATCH ATTACKS" episode in 2008, the *MonsterQuest* team appears to have been going all out to catch evidence of the creature that threw rocks at them earlier. I am going to discuss a more paranormal theory of rock throwing in a later section of the book but for now will stick to the unfolding of this *MonsterQuest* episode.

After the encouraging results from the hair morphology and DNA testing in the first episode and the rock-throwing incident, *MonsterQuest* developed a three-pronged strategy for capturing evidence of Sasquatch. First, they placed audio and video recorders in a custom-made blackout blind that would give the cabin the appearance of being quiet while someone was actually monitoring twenty-four seven. Second, the team installed camera traps with scent lures and electronic trackers all around the structure. Third, *MonsterQuest* mounted infrared cameras all around the outside of the building.

The team went in for a twelve-day mission and were there for several days with absolutely no activity. Doug Hajicek, in his *Sasquatch Chronicles* interview and on the show, theorized that the creatures may not have been in the area since the team arrived before the blueberries were ripe that year. When a sighting report came in from a First Nations reserve about one hundred fifteen miles south of their location, the *MonsterQuest* group decided to go check it out.

Helen Pahpasay and her mother were driving to a favourite blueberry-picking site on the Grassy Narrows Ojibway Reserve when they encountered something unknown in the road. In an interview with CBC News, the witness said:

> It was black, about eight feet long and all black, and the way it walked was upright, human-like, but more—I don't know how to describe it—more of a husky walk, I guess ... It didn't look normal.

Speaking to the Kenora *Miner and News*, Pahpasay noted:

> I thought I was seeing things, so I didn't say anything ... I looked over to my mom and she was rubbing her eyes ... It was just walking casually ... I know it wasn't an animal, cause it was upright. It was human like, like the way we walk ...

The creature seemed to recognize their attention and vanished into the woods. The two frightened women returned to their home, without picking a single berry, only to be dragged back out to the site by eager relatives. Randy Fobister, Pahpasay's brother, found a track that he immediately photographed and disseminated on the internet. Unusually, this track appeared to be of a six-toed Sasquatch, something that is supposed to be impossible for a primate.

The *MonsterQuest* team had little to add to the sighting reports as they appeared in the paper. A search of the site showed that the area was travelled extensively by bears, and Dr. Meldrum theorized that the track was simply two overlapping bear tracks. He could not state this definitively since there was also evidence that the track did not belong to a bear, specifically given the size of the outer toe. Another track might have been found near a juneberry bush in the area, but nothing conclusive came of this find.

Perhaps the biggest thing to come out of this second *MonsterQuest* episode was that the DNA analysis of the first season was called into question by another analysis, this one done by Dr. Mehrdad Hajibabaei at the University of Guelph. Hajibabaei was unable to duplicate Dr. Nelson's results from the first episode and theorized that Nelson's sample may have contained human contaminants. I will note, in passing, that the *MonsterQuest* team, after making a good start in their first episode, must have been very frustrated when their best efforts produced no results in the second episode. This frustration could relate to the more paranormal explanation of so-called Class B encounters that I will discuss in a later chapter.

As with so much Sasquatch evidence, things seem to become blurry as we look at them more closely. Let's return to some more eyewitness accounts.

———

THE SASQUATCH CANADA website gives the sighting report of Mr. and Mrs. D. Heibert accompanied by a remarkable photo shot with a Canon EOS Digital Rebel XT camera with a 300 mm lens. As I have noted, I don't wish to get into the constant back-and-forth about the authenticity of photos, but a look at this picture will cue the reader to some of the remarkable photo and video evidence coming out of Canada.

At 1439 hours on 15 April 2009, the Heiberts were at their cabin on a small lake just outside of Lady Evelyn Smoothwater Park in the Temagami region of Ontario. Mrs. Heibert went to open the blinds in the back bedroom and spotted a creature on the top of a hill approximately fifty to seventy yards away. She called to her husband, who picked up his camera and moved out to the back corner of the cabin in an attempt to photograph the creature. As he moved, the witness thinks that the creature saw him and froze.

As so often happens with photography of Sasquatch and other strange phenomenon, Mr. Heibert had some difficulty getting his camera ready to shoot. In his case, he had to delete photos from the SD card so that he would have room for any photos he shot of the animal. The witness moved quickly enough to get two photos of the creature initially and a later one. The pictures were taken from a position looking up the hill from the top of the cabin's propane tank.

"The thing stood perfectly still for what seemed like five minutes," Mr. Heibert stated. "I turned my head for a split second and it was gone." Sasquatch researchers often attribute these seeming disappearances to the forest giant's quick movement and ability to use camouflage, but we will see later sightings where a creature vanishes in front of the witness.

Mr. Heibert described the Sasquatch as at least ten feet tall and very massive, roughly twice his own size.

The sighting was reported to both the Ministry of Natural Resources (MNR) officers and provincial police and was, seemingly, laughed off. Interestingly, though, a game warden and several biologists from the MNR appeared later and "attended the cabin", taking photos and investigating. These officials even stayed on after the Heiberts left the cabin.

The incident shook Mrs. Heibert enough that the couple sold their cabin in 2010, and the *Sasquatch Canada* report notes that the sighting was the culmination of several odd incidents that occurred around the cabin, including a noise like a seismic thumper truck in the woods along with tree breaks in 2004, blue and black helicopters flying low and circling the area in 2006, and the blockage of a road to the cabin with large boulders in 2007.

Given the signs of Sasquatch activity followed by a sighting as well as the involvement of the MNR and those interesting helicopters, one begins to wonder what is going on in that section of the Canadian wilderness. Perhaps the government is taking more of an interest in these creatures than it wants to let on?

I can imagine that encountering something like what we see in the picture series might be traumatizing, but in the next report, we meet a young person who literally broke down after a frightening encounter.

———

IN AN ARTICLE TITLED "It's Face Was Literally Something Out of Hell" on the *Sasquatch Chronicles* blog, an anonymous listener details a frightening incident that still haunted them two years after the sighting. The witness was careful not to identify the area they were in, only saying it was Ontario, nor even their gender, so I will use the pronoun they in this report.

The witness was seventeen at the time of the episode and assisted with an Airsoft league in their area. For those unfamiliar, Airsoft is a game like paintball in which players tag each other out with pellets fired from a specially designed and often very realistic air gun. Airsoft games can range from historical re-enactment of battles to close-quarter combat simulations and require a playing field with structures and other "cover" for the opposing teams.

The witness was a co-commissioner of their league and tasked with structure repair and general clean-up of the designated play area, some of which was covered in dense forest but also included a creek and a bridge over the creek. The witness had finished tasks on one side of the bridge and crossed to the other side of the creek when they began hearing twigs snapping in the woods.

At first, the Airsoft player thought nothing of the sounds. They had spent time camping in the forest and knew that animals such as deer made such sounds. The witness continued with their job but noted that it was about 1930 hours and beginning to get dark. As the witness worked, however, the sound of footsteps multiplied until they felt that they were hearing footfalls from four different locations.

As so often happens in these cases, the witness began to have an "eerie" feeling and actually drew their Airsoft pistol. They knew that they could not really harm anyone with the air gun but thought that they might be able to scare a homeless person away with it.

The footsteps were then accompanied by a clicking sound that the witness was unable to identify, and as they tried to work out what they were hearing, a high-volume vocalization sounded from the woods. The sound was such that the witness felt their stomach drop and stated that they almost vomited.

The witness thought that they dropped to their knees, and when they looked up, "this tall black as night man/ape ... came forward and the face made me cry. Its face was literally something out of hell ..." The "beast" was at least ten feet tall and accompanied by three other smaller creatures. Certain that they were going to die, the witness took a couple of steps back.

The Sasquatch "screamed" again, and this broke the

witness' frightened freeze. They ran, as fast as they could, for the bridge across the creek. The creature pursued, and the witness, a cross-country athlete, stated that it took the animal no time to catch up to them. Interestingly, the animal remained "about a basketball court away" from the witness.

The witness crossed the bridge and felt that structure vibrate as the Sasquatch stepped on the other side. Rather than run straight for the main trail, the witness, for whatever reason, turned and started toward a ridge that led to a second entrance to the Airsoft play area. Glancing back down the trail they had avoided, the witness saw yet another creature materialize out of the cover along that trail. Their intuitive decision to turn onto the ridge had saved them from yet another run-in with one of these massive creatures.

The witness ran, full tilt and then some, back to their car and then sped home. In the aftermath of the incident, the witness suffered symptoms that we might recognize as PTSD:

[I] replayed the event over and over. For weeks I relived it every time I closed my eyes. The screams echoed through my head and I couldn't believe that it was real. I basically had a nervous breakdown.

While most Sasquatch sightings are benign, we do occasionally come across a sighting like this one where the witness is completely traumatized. One has only to listen to a podcast like *Sasquatch Chronicles* to hear of people who, after their encounter, refuse to ever go into the woods again or, at least, require companions to go with them. I think that the depth of these reactions, terrible as they are, argues forcibly for the reality of this phenomenon.

Additionally, looking at the behaviour of the Sasquatch group in this testimony, one wonders what would have happened to this witness if they had stayed on the main trail. I can't help but feel that the large creature chasing the witness was herding that person toward the creature waiting along the trail. What might have happened if the witness hadn't zigged when they were supposed to zag and had run in to the "moss-covered" animal down the main trail.

Another mysterious disappearance in the wilderness?

CHAPTER FOUR
SK, YUKON, NWT, NB, NS

SASKATCHEWAN

WHILE THE PROVINCE of Saskatchewan is best known for its southern prairies, the area also has woodland in the northern part of the province. Interestingly, some of the sparse Sasquatch reports that I located for this province took place in places where one might not expect to see the Hairy One. I will comment on this as we go through the section.

As noted, however, there are woodland sections of Saskatchewan, and our first tale takes place in a logging area. In an article titled "Some Doubt, Some Believe, Some Aren't Sure", journalist Joe Frazier tells the story of a sighting in 1974. Jack Cochran, a logging crane operator on Fir Mountain, was looking through the boom of his crane on an April morning. The structure of the boom obstructed his view, but he saw "two long legs walking toward the timber".

The crane operator wondered what one of his colleagues was doing in the area and then looked again. He realized that he was not looking at a person, and a "cold chill" went up the back of his neck. "Whatever Cochran saw had huge shoulders and walked upright with a gliding motion into the timber". The logger told his co-workers outright that he had seen a "Bigfoot", but they told him that he had gotten too much sun.

A day later, one of Cochran's cohorts, Fermin Osborne, spotted "some kind of monster". Amusingly, the paper reports that Osborne was "from the South" and rather hotheaded. The man followed the creature that he saw to the "brink of a hill" and then tried to get it to turn and look at him by rolling rocks down after it. The creature never turned, but Cochran reported that Osborne told him, "Jack, I guess you weren't crazy because I saw it too."

A later examination of the area found rocks that had been rolled down the hill and others that had been pressed into the ground as if by a great weight.

Robin Tarnowetski, reporting on the *SaskToday* website, notes that nearby Rockglen was the site of several sightings of a Sasquatch-like creature during the 1970s. Local residents referred to the creature as Zoobie or Zoobs and stated that it stood eight to ten feet tall, had a "high voice" and carried a skunk's odour. While no details are given about the sightings, it is interesting to note that Rockglen is less than an hour by car from Fir Mountain.

———

AND THEN THERE are the sightings of the Hairy One that do not occur in the dense forests of Canada.

In 2005, near the town of Wakaw, a duck hunter had a sighting in a mixed area of marshes, hills, and many small patches of trees. The area had some cover, but this seems an unlikely setting for the forest giant. At the end of this section, we will see another Saskatchewan sighting where the creature seemed to be out on open prairie.

It should also be noted that, while dense forest land seems to be the Sasquatch's favourite habitat, these beings have also been spotted in the Arizona deserts as well as in the Dakotas on the Lakota reservations. Neither area is noted for extensive cover, and this observation should give us pause when making conclusions about the nature of these animals.

In BFRO report #12733, an individual out duck hunting made a gruesome discovery while making his way through rain-soaked fields to a favourite shooting pond. The fields were freshly cut, and swaths of plant material lay around the field. Sighting a flash of white under one of the swaths, the hunter lifted the plants away to discover seven dead terns (a type of seabird) packed together in a "big lump" and showing no external signs of injury.

The hunter didn't know what to think of his find but, assuming that raccoons had somehow stashed the birds for a later meal, moved on to his hunting site and bagged several ducks. The witness decided to depart when the rain started back up but promptly got his truck stuck in the mud and had to dismount to go seek help.

As the witness made his way along a road that connected to the trail where the truck was stuck, he had his head down, trying to keep the rain out of his eyes, when he caught movement in his peripheral vision. The witness described the event as follows:

> I saw something ... it didn't seem really tall ... but I was a couple hundred yards away from it ... but it was big ... I mean real big ... wide across the shoulders and no neck just like a big giant head sittin on huge shoulders and short little legs and long arms it was moving extremely fast but not running ... it was heading down the ditch at this little valley I was walking through ... I saw it for 3 or 4 strides then it disap-

peared into some trees that were at the bottom ... the valley was very narrow but also very long and trees cover the whole bottom of it ... it freaked me out ... it had to have crossed the road right in front of me but I had my head down and didn't see it till it had crossed the road and was heading into the valley-bottom.

When the witness arrived at the spot where the creature must have passed, he found a single footprint, sixteen inches long and five to six inches wide, in the muddy sand along the shoulder of the road. The witness further noted that the creature was a dark brownish reddish colour.

The witness wondered, since the pile of dead birds he found were only a few hundred yards from the top of the valley where the creature disappeared, if the terns were not a food cache for the Sasquatch. He also noted that he had heard of no other Sasquatch reports in the area and that he was very reluctant to share his sighting for fear of ridicule.

MOVING BACK to the woodland of northern Saskatchewan, the Saskatoon *Star-Phoenix* covered an interesting story from the area around Torch Lake.

In December 2006, twenty-year-old Shaylane Beatty was driving from Deschambault Lake after Christmas shopping. Her sighting occurred in the daytime, during a bright afternoon, and as so often happens, the young woman thought she was seeing a bear when she first noticed movement on the side of the road.

As she came closer, however, the witness found that the creature was walking on two legs along the forest edge near Torch Lake. The being was described as approximately two and a half metres (just over eight feet) tall and muscular, with long "floppy" arms and broad shoulders. The creature was covered with dark hair and was unlike anything Beatty had ever seen before.

The witness was so shocked by her sighting that she lost concentration on her driving and nearly swerved into a ditch. The newspaper reports don't mention what happened to the Sasquatch, but Beatty obviously returned home and spoke of the event.

The next day, she and two uncles went back to the site and discovered a trackway that consisted of over a hundred footprints, which measured over fifty centimetres (over 19.5 inches) in length. Pictures were taken, but Jeff Meldrum, the anthropologist who studies Sasquatch tracks, didn't have a definite opinion on their origin. While the tracks were within the size range seen with other alleged Sasquatch tracks, Meldrum noted that, "given the quality of the photographs, it's impossible to render any meaningful analysis".

Meldrum did find the sighting combined with physical evidence compelling, and the *Star-Phoenix* article quotes Beatty as saying, "my uncles were struggling to walk through the same snow the Sasquatch just breezed through". The witness also noted that the two uncles could not even begin to match the creature's stride, even when they tried jumping to do so.

Roadside sightings are extremely common, and I will be giving further examples and some discussion later in the book. Given the rarity of sightings in Saskatchewan, I am going to cover another roadside sighting in the next story.

━━━

I MENTIONED PREVIOUSLY that we would see another Sasquatch in an unlikely area. In the *Global News*, we find the brief report of a video shot near Craven, Saskatchewan. According to the report and the caption to the YouTube video (link in the bibliography) posted in January of 2014, a family were out for a drive when they sighted an unusual animal on the side of the road. They immediately stopped their car and shot video of the creature as it disappeared into some tree cover in a gulley along the side of the highway.

The video seems to show a very broad-shouldered being moving purposefully off the road and down into the gulley. The head appears to have the conical shape of the classic Sasquatch, and the creature appears to be quite massive. The being's movements seem very fluid, and what we can see of the creature appears to be a uniform dark colour.

I've stated that I will refrain from video analysis throughout the book, but, given that the video is evidence of a visual sighting, I feel compelled to discuss why such evidence is so fraught for myself and other researchers/investigators.

The first thing that springs to mind in examining this footage is the location. This film was taken deep within the prairie section of Saskatchewan, and though the subject of the film seems to have found temporary cover, there is no place for the forest hide-and-seek antics of the Sasquatch on the great prairies. While it is known that the creatures have been sighted in desert scapes and other low-cover areas, I have to wonder why an animal that is notorious for its reclusiveness would expose itself so. It almost seems that a Sasquatch in an area like this would need supernatural powers to stay out of sight.

The other thing that we need to examine when looking at the film is whether this could be a person. We have no idea what range the film was taken at, and no effort appears to have been made to establish the size of the being in the video. Whatever is being filmed is walking in tall grass, so we can only see the figure from the waist up. Might this not simply be a large, broad-shouldered man in a hoodie (thus the seemingly conical head)? If that is so, was this a hoax being played on the family, or might the film itself be a hoax?

I have no way to know definitively if this is a film of a Sasquatch or not, and therefore, I have no desire to get caught up in the endless debates about videos like these. What we see in such films is coloured by our perception. A Sasquatch enthusiast might try to prove that this was, indeed, a film of the Hairy One while the so-called skeptics will always find a way to "debunk" the film, claiming it is a large man in a ghillie suit, for instance. Rather than spend time on this constant push and pull, I would rather spend time collecting stories and listening to witnesses.

YUKON

There are a number of reports out of the Yukon, but many of them are roadside sightings, which I will try to group into another chapter. One notable sighting, covered in the Ottawa *Citizen,* took place in Teskin, a small town of four hundred or so people, in 2005. According to the residents interviewed, there were numerous sightings of a Sasquatch creature throughout their little town.

Melvin Harper reported that the night was quiet on the evening of his sighting. He began to hear branches crackling, and the neighbourhood dogs set up a din. Harper saw a figure "flitting" past his neighbour's light post before making its way through a forested area near the log homes in the area. Harper is quoted as saying, "It was something big, about eight-feet-tall. It's black, hairy muscular. It was huge ... He was like teasing us, making noises in the bush, coming back and forth."

Another witness, Tom Dickson, stated that the creature was "like how you seen it on TV, how they advertise it". He stated that he could not see the eyes of the animal but that it was moving fast. He likened the shock of seeing it to the shock of encountering a bear unexpectedly.

The article mentions that at least three sightings of the creature had occurred in Teslin during that year and goes on to give the testimony of Roger Smarch. Smarch only heard the animal crashing through the brush, but when he went out to examine the spot where he had heard something large in the woods, he found crushed flowers and saplings snapped in half more than two metres (about 6.5 feet) up their trunks.

Smarch also discovered a deep footprint in mud, over thirty centimetres (eleven inches) in length. His three-hundred-pound uncle tried to make a track of that depth in the mud and failed. It should be noted that local hunters didn't find the track all that convincing, stating that it could be the print of a moose that slipped in the mud. Smarch was not convinced and also recovered hair from the scene. Unfortunately, later analysis of the sample seemed to indicate that it was from a bear, which would explain the heavy crashing sound and even the track (bear tracks are often taken for Sasquatch tracks, according to people like Jeff Meldrum).

Even if the noise and tracks are not definitive, we still have the eyewitness testimony of several people. Another Smarch, Rodney, and his friend Alex Lindsay had an uncomfortable encounter with the creature when it was said to have banged on the side of a relative's house where they were staying. Looking out into the early morning, they stated that they saw the being hiding behind a car, its knees jutting up over the vehicle. I find this description almost comical, but the two boys apparently found it quite terrifying.

It's interesting to note that ninety percent of the population of Teslin is Tlingit, a First Nations group that has references in its lore to a being they call the bushman—a sort of boogeyman designed to keep children from wandering too far from settlements. I'll have more to say about Native beliefs about Sasquatch in a later chapter.

NORTHWEST TERRITORIES

Falling out of one's canoe does not seem like it would be a life-threatening event. But when one is alone in the frigid waters of the Northwest Territories Tlicho region, it certainly can be. And when one encounters a "bushman" during the struggle for survival, the episode becomes even more frightening.

In an article cited by the *Sasquatch Chronicles* blog, we hear the story of forty-two-year-old Tony Williah, who was boating from Whati to the northern tip of Lac La Martre. Williah's ordeal began when he spotted some garbage in the water and attempted to retrieve it. An unexpected wave sent him over the side of his boat.

Williah, of course, tried to pull himself back into the boat but could not manage it against the weight of his waterlogged clothes. Finally, in desperation, the man grabbed a plastic bag of supplies and set off for shore.

The exhausted witness managed to swim to an island and pull himself up on shore, but his rest was short-lived. "All of the sudden, there was a big man standing beside me," Williah is quoted as saying, "he must have walked away because I heard some branches break throughout the bushes ..."

Tired as he was, Williah was not going to spend time on an island occupied by a being he identified as a bushman. He "packed his clothes in a white bag and readied [himself] to leave". The fatigued man swam away from the island and ended up being alone in the wilderness for another forty-eight hours before being rescued by the RCMP and Canadian military.

Apparently, he was quite willing to tell anyone who would listen about his encounter with a bushman.

While brief, this story highlights the fear factor involved in sighting a Sasquatch. This man was in desperate straits. Even in July, when this event happened, night-time temperatures dip between ten and fifteen degrees Celsius (fifty to sixty degrees Fahrenheit). Soaking wet after a dunk in a frigid lake, such temps can bring on hypothermia in a matter of minutes. Yet this witness, after seeing the "bushman", got himself together and went back into the water rather than spend time drying off and perhaps warming himself.

From the far west of Canada, let's now look at some stories from the Atlantic provinces.

NEW BRUNSWICK

The following account, from the *Phantoms and Monsters* blog, is short enough to quote in its entirety:

Grand Falls, New Brunswick, Canada: "My name is Bob. I've been in the woods all my life and most of what you talk about has happened to me at some point although I have never had as close an encounter as you have had. Me and a few friends were hunting back in 1986 and were sweeping through a fresh cut area near Grand Falls, New Brunswick, Canada and spotted something walking on two legs at about 400 yards from us. We watched this thing for close to a half hour walk horizontally across a ridgeline of pretty open hardwood in front of us and your description of the forearms was dead on through my scope. I could tell how big its arms were. Transfixed for days after that, we all never told really anybody about it. We figured they would think we were nuts but all my time being in the woods; the knocks, the whistles, and thrown objects were there ...

Four hundred yards is a considerable distance, but it seems clear that this witness observed the creature for an extended period of time and did have access to his rifle scope, which would have given him a much clearer view. I could wish that the observer had provided more detail about what the animal was doing and its overall appearance, but it is often the case that witnesses get "target locked" on a particular aspect of the phenomenon they are observing and cannot give a full recounting of events. As I've noticed previously, seeing such a being can cause the human mind to react with shock.

I found several sighting reports in New Brunswick, but almost all were roadside events, which I will discuss later. Still, this report and the next make it clear that Sasquatch are seen in New Brunswick, and the creature seems to follow its normal hide-and-seek pattern there.

IN REPORT #7353 from the *BFRO* website, witness Steve D gives his account of events that transpired in the summer of 1998 around July or August. This witness lived in the Ottawa area at the time but was on vacation, visiting friends in Red Banks (New Brunswick) when he decided to take a solo motorcycle trip into Kouchibougac Provincial Park.

After rising in the morning, the witness decided to avail himself of the trails in the park and chose one that led to a large bog and accompanying observation tower. He recalled the bog as being the biggest he had ever seen, one and a half kilometres wide by three-quarters of a kilometre.

Seemingly quite impressed by the bog, Steve D climbed

the observation tower so that he could further observe the "spectacular view". He was particularly interested in animal spotting, and as he looked about, he spotted something unknown to him.

About five hundred feet away, directly in front of him, a greyish-brown creature was walking away from him. The witness stated firmly that he never considered that it might be a man as "its colouring was too close to its surrounding and too uniform". The animal was walking upright, and Steve D continued to watch it, "desperate to get an identification", until it left his view.

The witness descended the tower and walked along the boardwalk toward where he had seen the animal. He considered going into the bog after the thing, but "fear of the unknown" caused him to reconsider.

Before leaving the area, however, he ascended the observation tower again and had a second sighting of the creature. The unknown animal was walking from left to right this time, and "it was close enough that I could see the light between its legs as it walked and noticed its lower leg and arms seemed longer than a humans".

The creature seemed to be collecting something from the ground as it walked, and the witness noted that it didn't need to bend over to pick things up. Steve D watched the being for about twenty minutes during this observation and made the interesting comment that he felt like he was watching a shadow. He also made the odd observation that he felt that the animal knew that he did not have binoculars or a camera so that he could take a closer look at it.

Well-known BFRO investigator Matt Moneymaker followed up on the sighting and homed in on the comment about watching a shadow. Steve D explained that he used this metaphor simply to demonstrate the complete uniformity of the creature's colour and that nothing further should be read into the statement.

Moneymaker also noted that the witness believed the collecting behaviour was likely the picking of berries and flowers on low-lying plants. The creature did not bend over but, instead, bent its knees to collect these possible food sources.

Steve D seemed to have a lot of connection to the creature that he was observing. As Moneymaker reported:

> The animal went about its business without paying Steve much attention. Steve's sense was that it left his view initially not because it was frightened of him, but rather because it didn't want to cause a fear reaction in him. When it saw that Steve wasn't going to react with fear, it wasn't bothered. This was just Steve's feeling at the time, which he still stands by, and is entirely possible.

How would the creature know what Steve D was feeling? Or better yet, how would the witness seem to know what the creature thought about him? While most of the cases I encountered in Canada seemed to be simple observations of an unknown animal, even here, there are hints of something stranger attached to the Sasquatch phenomenon. I will be discussing this further in later sections.

In the meantime, let's move on to the province of Nova Scotia.

NOVA SCOTIA

A Thornburn *Post* newspaper article from 1913 gives us an indication that Sasquatch may have been present on the peninsula of Nova Scotia for some time. Reporter Frank Johnson tells us:

In sleepy backwaters of Picton County, something has been raiding chicken coops and stealing milk from the cows. Mrs. Ervin MacKay, a resident of Marsh Road ... told this writer that "There is something evil out there. Something big and shadowy and it scares the bejeebers out of me". A tour of the area yielded a large number of footprints, which were very large, up to 15 inches in length and were clearly made by something heavy. Mavis Merriweather, a local widower, told us that the creature comes from the Marsh at night and retreats there before dawn. She further stated that, "That great beast carried off my beau three fortnights ago, and he hasn't been seen since. It's scary up here at night alone, you know," she explained. Upon review of local historical documents, it seems the beast its [sic] seen for a year or two every fifty years. It comes, causes a ruckus, and then is gone. In this reporter's opinion, it [sic] best to leave such mysteries alone, and hope no harm comes to those living nearby ...

I find that last a little disingenuous since the widow had already reported the disappearance of her "beau". It seems to me that this would have been a grand case for investigation with mysterious disappearances and the "stealing of milk from cows". Given that the only way milk leaves a cow is through calves suckling or being milked, one wonders how a Sasquatch, if that is what this was, managed to take milk.

There is a section in my book *Canadian Monsters and Mysteries* that deals with faery lore. Nova Scotia is rife with these tales, and I cannot help but note that stealing milk is also something attributed to faeries in their lore. Again, the mechanism for these thefts is mysterious.

For a more modern account, let's look at the testimony of Chris.

———

A GUEST NAMED CHRIS, speaking on *Bigfoot Eyewitness Radio*, had a couple of close encounters with the Hairy One during his childhood in Nova Scotia. The witness made a point of stating, as he introduced himself, that he was a truck driver and had driven all over the United States and Canada. He also performed music part-time and was an "animal lover" who knew the creatures of his area.

In 1972, Chris' cousin was visiting, so the two went to sit out on the front porch of his home. As they sat there, the pair noticed four black creatures crossing a field about a quarter of a mile away. Two of the subjects were larger, and Chris noted that they stayed on two legs the entire time he was seeing them. The other two creatures were smaller and would sometimes drop to all fours but then pop back up to resume bipedal locomotion.

Chris was certain that the beings were not bears since they did not move like bears, a testimony that we hear often in Sasquatch lore. The witness and his cousin observed the animals for three to four minutes before they disappeared into the forest. Chris stated that if these creatures were not Sasquatch, he did not know what they were because they certainly weren't bears.

Later that year, Chris was riding his dirt bike on a motor-cycle trail. Unexplainably, a white stone had been left on the trail. The witness stopped his motorcycle, got off and picked up the rock, turning it over in his hand and wondering how it had gotten there. Chris had a "sixth sense" to turn around and spotted a Sasquatch not fifteen feet behind him, moving from one clump of trees to another.

Startled, Chris said that he screamed, and the creature went behind a tree, remaining motionless although Chris could still see its legs. The creature was dull black or grey in colour.

Slowly, the witness made his way over to his waiting bike. He had a different angle to view the creature and noted that he could see the breeze blowing its hair. Without taking his eyes off the Sasquatch, Chris remounted and "hauled ass" out of the location.

Chris is one of those people whom I believe benefited from what author Gavin De Becker calls the gift of fear. De Becker, a long-time executive protection professional, maintains that, while our brain filters the mass of perceptual information that we process every second, it is also acutely aware of everything going on in our environment.

When we have that deep feeling that something is not right or that a person is a threat, De Becker maintains that we should listen to these signals. In his book *The Gift of Fear: Listening to the Intuition that Protects Us from Danger,* he gives many examples of people who were victims of violent crimes who might not have been if they had listened to that feeling of wrongness.

In the case of Chris, we see a young person who had a "sixth sense" that he needed to turn around. We have no way of knowing what the being's intentions were, but when we look at First Nations beliefs about the Sasquatch, we will see that the indigenous people believed that these creatures sometimes stole children. Given the speed with which these beings are said to move, Chris might have been in some danger. The witness believes that his quick turn startled the creature. That startled effect seems to have given the witness time to remount and make his escape.

In an interesting postscript to his story, Chris told the host that the 1972 sightings in the area were all credited to "abnormally large bears". These "bears" were seen crossing roads with armloads of corn, walking on two legs, but Chris noted that the people of the area were tight-lipped about anything they did not understand.

The witness also noted that hunters in the area had heard strange noises, like those made by a human infant. These sounds were also attributed to bears. Chris himself had noticed a strange odour along the tree line, one that was very strong in one place but disappeared if one took a couple of steps beyond that spot. As a side note, scent does not generally appear and then abruptly disappear from one step to the next.

Finally, Chris noted that his grandfather had heard sounds like the infamous "samurai chatter" while out in the woods. The grandfather was a hunting guide but still could not identify the source of the sounds. During this time period, when Chris stayed with his grandparents, something would get on the porch of the house, something heavy enough to shake the entire structure. Chris was forbidden from looking to see what it was and told to just go back to bed.

While Chris' experience made him more cautious in the woods, Earl's sighting sparked a lifelong interest in these creatures.

———

IN A WITNESS REPORT from the *Sasquatch Canada* website, Earl tells of seeing a Sasquatch as it made its way through alder trees in Nova Scotia.

I am an avid amateur photographer and have always loved hiking and exploring. Nature has always fascinated me. Even as young children my brother and I would camp for days with almost no food or supplies to "test" ourselves in a remote wooded area. I remember clearly, finding what I can only describe as a nest large enough for us both to climb inside but the eerie feelings we got had us getting out of there ... We lived on Cape Breton Island ... I did see what I believe to be a Sasquatch.

I was 12 years old and did not see it's [sic] face but I did see it walking through Alders and although it was twilight I did get a clear view. It was walking and moving the brush with its hands and grabbing as it walked slightly hunched. I was frozen in a squatted position for at least a minute till it was far away enough for me to not be seen. I still have a clear memory of that evening and have been fascinated ever since. I've heard the term "here he goes again" so many times, every time the word Sasquatch comes out of my mouth. I'm 48 and to this day, every time I go into the woods, any woods, I always stay aware of my surroundings.

Applying a little math, Earl's sighting happened in 1976. As a nature buff, one would expect him to know what he was looking at and not mistake a bear for a Sasquatch. The detail of the creature "walking and moving brush with its hands and grabbing" seems to militate against a bear sighting. Bears do not have hands, and they certainly don't walk along on their hind legs, moving brush aside as they go.

It is interesting that one person encountering a Sasquatch becomes more cautious in the woods, if they will even return at all, while others who have the experience become quite obsessed with the experience and even seek to repeat it. This dichotomy in reactions to seeing a Sasquatch is yet another mystery that surrounds these creatures.

We are coming closer to the end of our tour of Canada. As with Nova Scotia, Sasquatch sightings are not common in Quebec, but they do happen. We will look at some sightings from Quebec and then move on to Newfoundland and Labrador.

CHAPTER FIVE
QUEBEC, LABRADOR AND NEWFOUNDLAND

QUEBEC

WES GERMER'S *Sasquatch Chronicles* podcast is a wealth of witness accounts, ranging from the terrifying to mysterious roadside encounters. In episode 191, Germer speaks to a witness about a sighting he had sometime between 1996 and 1998.

The witness, named Steve, was visiting the family home in St. Étienne de Bolton. As he usually did, the witness, who was then thirteen years old, and his nine-year-old cousin went down to the creek located behind the house. When they reached the creek, however, both boys froze.

There, sitting on the bank of the creek, was a "grayish white monstrous sized thing". Steve's first impression was that he was looking at a "elderly thin polar bear", but he realized quickly that this simply could not be the case. His other thought was that it looked something like one of the grey gorillas from the movie *Congo*.

When the creature began to turn its head, presumably toward the two boys, Steve wasted no time in rushing his cousin back up the trail and back to the house. As so often happens, when the boys related what they had seen, they were told that it was a large dog and advised to forget about it.

Steve never did forget the incident despite its brevity. In the written caption to the episode, the host quotes Steve as saying:

> It definitely wasn't a dog, or polar bear. The thing I remember the most are its shoulders. They were bony and decrepit. That's the only way I can describe it. It was like I was looking at the back and shoulders of a very large and hairy 95 year old man.

I found this sighting intriguing because it is one of the few sightings I encountered where the creature did not seem to be either a skinny adolescent or a robust adult. If the Sasquatch is, indeed, a relict hominid or unknown ape species, then it makes sense that there would be older members of the species sighted on occasion.

In 2012 and 2013, there were a couple of sightings by First Nations people in northern Quebec that caught my attention.

___

NUNAVIK IS an area of Quebec north of the 55th parallel, and it was the location of a reported sighting in 2012. According to the CBC News website, Maggie Cruikshank Qingalik of Akulivik was out with a friend picking berries when they saw something they could not explain.

Qingalik said at first, they thought it was another person picking berries. Then they noticed it was covered in long, dark hair. She said it was walking upright along the side of a hill and was taking long strides. They said it would also sometimes crawl.

"We weren't sure what it was at first. It was not a human being, it was really tall, and kept coming towards our direction and we could tell it was not human," she said.

The witness estimated the creature's height at ten to fifteen feet, and pictures of alleged tracks found at the site measured forty centimetres (almost 16 inches). Qingalik stated that she did not feel the animal was vicious, rather, it seemed to have no interest in the two berry pickers.

Still, the episode frightened the two women badly enough for them to leave the area and head home. They were said to have warned others about the sighting once they returned to their community.

CBC contacted an expert, of course, who immediately homed in on the height estimate and the size of the alleged tracks, calling both measurements exaggerated. This sort of thing really gets my goat. Who declared that, as this expert stated, Sasquatch range from six and a half feet to eight feet? This might be a good average from a number of witness sightings, but it is not a reason to discount a witness' height estimate.

The average Caucasian male is 5 feet, 9.6 inches. I am 6 feet, 7 inches. Are reports of my height exaggerated because I do not fall within the "norm"?

This is the sort of silliness that we see from so-called experts in a field where no one really knows what a Sasquatch is.

ANOTHER CBC NEWS ARTICLE, titled "Bigfoot sighting reported by Cree hunter near Wemindji, Que.", detailed an episode that happened in 2013. As the article notes, this encounter happened near Wemindji, a town of about 2,500 not far from the 55th parallel and the Nunavik section of Quebec.

Melvin Georgekish was driving his truck along a road near his town when he spotted two pairs of red eyes peering out of the woodland at him. He drove past the eyes but then decided to turn back and, when he arrived at the spot, shone his headlights on the area where he had seen the eyes. There was nothing there.

While skeptics might dismiss this as just another case of eye shine, Georgekish's reaction to the sighting is telling. As he put it, "I was thinking and thinking, and there's no animal that has red eyes over here. I am a hunter, and I've never seen something like that."

The witness returned to the location the next day and found footprints unlike any he had seen before in the moss. There were two prints, one measuring twenty centimetres (nine inches approximately) and the other thirty-five centimetres (almost fourteen inches). An accompanying photo showed Georgekish's foot well inside the track with the forefoot much larger and wider than the human foot, though toes, as on a human foot, seem to be plainly visible.

While this is not the strongest sighting in this book, I found Mr. Georgekish's encounter interesting for two reasons.

First, the witness' reaction to this event seems all out of proportion with the incident itself. The article notes that Georgekish "tossed and turned all night" contemplating the source of that eye shine and could not relate what he saw to a local animal he was familiar with. This certitude drove him back out to the spot where he had seen the eyes and led to his subsequent track find.

I spoke, in the story of Chris, about an intuition that may have saved that young man from further disturbance by a Sasquatch along the motorcycle trail he was travelling. Reading this hunter's reaction to what many would have dismissed as "some critter in the woods", makes me wonder if Mr.

Georgekish wasn't having an intuitive knowledge that he was seeing something more than a pair of raccoons in the brush.

The second interesting thing in this article is a small note from another Georgekish, Bradley, who told CBC news that "legends of Bigfoot are part of Cree oral history" and that the creatures are regarded as protectors of the Cree. I will have a good bit more to say about First Nations beliefs about Sasquatch, but this statement should spark interest. It is obvious that the Cree are aware of these beings and have assigned them meaning in their culture.

In the next section, we will look at another 2013 sighting in Quebec.

SASQUATCH SOMETIMES SEEM to establish themselves in an area and stay for a period of time. An anonymous witness reported such an event to the *Sasquatch Canada* website. In this case, the evidence for the presence of the Hairy One mounted until the witness had a visual sighting.

The first indication that there was something unusual going on at the property occurred as the witness was cleaning up his yard as winter thawed into spring. He had been out raking when he noticed an area of disturbed snow under a large pine tree and then spotted a handprint in a spot where the branches of the tree formed a sort of shelter against falling snow.

The witness stated that the handprint was approximately thirteen by thirteen inches. He took pictures but stated that the photos did not show the precision of the print. "The detail in the print was quite something. It was not just a flat print. You could see the texture in the palm like where the thumb muscle came down and what looked like calluses at the point where the fingers connect to the hand."

Over a period of two years after this event, the witness found footprints on the property that measured fourteen inches by six and a half inches with a stride length of about forty-six to fifty-four inches. The witness theorized that the animal kept returning because of several fruit trees on the property. He then went on to outline incidences of spotting eye shine, hearing vocalizations and rock clacking and the complete absence of deer, which had been common, on the property during the noted time period. Additionally, the witness' dogs and cats all reacted to something on the property at points throughout the given time frame.

The witness had seen something tall and dark moving through the spruce trees in the yard but had not had a clear sighting until he went out at night, between 2200 and 2300 hours. He was quietly smoking a cigar and enjoying the silence of the night when he heard "something that drew [his] attention to [his] neighbour's yard across the street". The witness likened the sound to Marge Simpson, the cartoon character, muttering, and stated that it was "gruff but feminine sounding in pitch".

The maker of the sound wandered from the neighbour's yard, into the witness' yard and then back to the neighbour's. When a figure first came into view, the witness thought it was his neighbour and took a few steps off the porch before realization hit him.

It was then I realized it was not the neighbour nor was it human. It was always my thinking that if I actually ever saw it my first reaction would be fear and that I would immediately run for cover when in reality there was absolutely no fear. None whatsoever that was surprise number one. Number two, I always imagined the hair being dull and shaggy like you see in tv and books. It was quite the contrary. The hair was long and glistened. To this day I don't know if its hair was wet but ... and here goes another funny comparison, it looked like a giant "cousin it" from the Addams family. The glistening hair was not at all what I expected. It was between 7 and 8 feet tall, no distinguishable neck from my perspective and as it crossed my lot I could see it from the side. The other thing that really hit me was the size of its shoulder. It was at least as big as my hip and very muscular looking. All the while it crossed over without making a sound. Not a twig snap, not rustling the grass, nothing. Almost as if it floated through. All this happened in the space of about 15 seconds although reliving it, it seemed much longer.

The witness bolted for the house, where he retrieved his camera and began taking blind shots with the flash in hopes of catching something. While he did not get a photo of the creature, interestingly, almost all activity ceased after this attempt to photograph the creature.

The Manwolf or Dogman is notoriously camera shy, as I note in my book *Canadian Monsters and Mysteries*. Perhaps Sasquatch is as well?

LABRADOR

Stories of Sasquatch or, at least, Sasquatch-like creatures in Labrador seem to fall mostly in the historical realm and, in First Nations lore, seem to intermingle with stories of the Little People and other faery-like beings.

Bruce Hynes, in his book *Here Be Dragons* about strange creatures in Newfoundland and Labrador, tells us of several interesting First Nations legends, including the Inuit legend of the *Tuniit*, a race of people regarded as both ancestors and devils or spirits. These beings were said to be much stronger than a human and to have very long arms and legs.

The beings were said to live in caves in the Torngat Mountain region but, paradoxically, were also known to live in stone houses amongst the Inuit people. The Tuniit were personified as giant white bears but were clearly delineated from the known polar bear species. They used stone implements but were best known for stealing items that they could not make, such as kayaks and bows. Such behaviour was tolerated due to the great size and strength of the creatures.

Eventually, however, the Thule people, ancestors of the Inuit, rose up against the Tuniit and hunted them to near extinction; it was believed that some Tuniit survived into the 1930s, living in the remote fastnesses of the Torngat Mountains.

Amongst the Innu, the easternmost band of First Nations people known as the Cree, there is a being known simply as the Hairy Creature. Hynes notes that there is both a Hairy Creature Lake and a Hairy Creature Mountain in Labrador. Both sites have stories attached to them.

At *Kaminaushit-natuashu*, Hairy Creature Lake, fifty kilometres west-southwest of Nain, a hunter was said to have disappeared, along with his entire dog team from the area. Members of the band were warned to avoid the area, "presumably because of the presence of a hairy and evil being".

Kaminaushitm upishkutinam, Hairy Creature Mountain, about twelve kilometres from the lake, is the site of an Innu folktale in which a tribal member saw a "human-like creature on the promontory. It was hairy, large, and threatening, and the observer made great haste to leave the area ..." As with the Tuniit of the Inuit, some believe that the Hairy Creature no longer exists.

The tales of the Innu also include a strange being called the *Uapanatsheu*, or "sneaking creatures", a mostly invisible presence that loved to steal from traps and throw stones or sticks at Innu tents. Naturally, there is an *Uapanatsheu-nipi*, or

Sneaking Creature Lake, eighty kilometres southeast of Happy Valley-Goose Bay. Intriguingly, Hynes relates the story of Lizette Penashue's great-great-grandmother whose dogs treed a sneaking creature. Rather than kill the being, this Innu ancestor kept it alive, but, as with all these stories, we have no further details of what happened to the sneaking creature nor any photographs or other evidence of its presence amongst the Innu.

It seems that, even when they are captured or killed, Sasquatch or whatever the sneaking creature was have a talent for disappearing into history without leaving any trace.

WHILE THE FIRST NATIONS people certainly told tales of creatures that could be Sasquatch, the European settlers also encountered strange things. In an interesting article from *Beachcombing's Bizarre History Blog,* the author of the blog relates a story that came from the memoirs of Dr. Wilfrid Thomason Grenfell.

[O]ne year while visiting at the head of Hamilton Inlet, a Scotch settler came aboard to ask my advice about a large animal that had appeared round his house. Though he had sat up night after night with his gun, he had never seen it. His children had seen it several times disappearing into the trees. The French agent of Revillon Freres, twenty miles away, had come over, and together they had tracked it, measured the footmarks in the mud, and even fenced some of them round. The stride was about eight feet, the marks as of the cloven hoofs of an ox. The children described the creature as looking like a huge hairy man; and several nights the dogs had been driven growling from the house into the water. Twice the whole family had heard the creature prowling around the cottage, and tapping at the doors and windows. The now grown-up children persist in saying that they saw this wild thing. Their house is twenty miles up the large Grand River, and a hundred and fifty miles from the coast.

The so-called skeptics (a skeptic is actually supposed to approach a problem with an open mind) have dismissed this sighting as a moose because of the massive stride length and appearance of cloven-hoofed tracks. As often happens, these debunkers fail to take several items of the testimony into account.

First, the children described the creature as looking like a hairy man. A child who grew up in this area would certainly know what a moose looked like, so I am loathe to discard the testimony of eyewitnesses over tracks. Second, while a wandering moose might provoke a reaction from the family dogs, depending on their courage, moose most assuredly do not tap on doors and windows. Finally, the assumption is that the track line was produced by the mysterious creatures. Unless someone saw that animal making the tracks, it is entirely possible that the tracks were indeed produced by a moose and the two incidents were simply conflated.

Even if we discard the testimony of these witnesses, there is still another, dramatic sighting from the Labrador area.

IN ANOTHER INTERESTING SETTLER STORY, Bruce Hynes tells the tale of William Decker, "a resident of one of the numerous small settlements at the extreme northern end of the Great Northern Peninsula. In 1895, Decker set off on a hunting trip that led him into the "boggy southwest hinterlands of Pistolet

Bay". The hunter was making his way across the "frozen quag-mire" when he was "startled by an unearthly cry".

The man turned to face the sound and was terrified to see an "immense beast-man" moving toward him in "tremendous bounds". Decker had time to do nothing more than point his muzzleloader and pull the trigger, as the creature was already at frighteningly close range.

The firearm brought the creature down, but it soon managed to get back to its feet. The hunter had just enough time to reload and fired again, dropping the animal so close to him that he could smell its "foetid breath". Decker was a cautious man. He rammed home another charge and took a third shot at the creature before determining that it was, finally, dead.

The hunter took some approximate measurements. The creature was three and a half metres tall with an arm span of four metres (approximately eleven and a half feet with an arm span of slightly over thirteen feet). Decker estimated the weight at about four hundred and fifty kilograms (about nine hundred ninety-two pounds). The animal was covered in long, dark hair, and its tracks were so large that they dwarfed Decker's feet, even with snowshoes on.

It certainly seems that William Decker had an encounter with a Sasquatch, but as always happens in these cases (so far), the body was never recovered, and this downed Sasquatch disappeared, along with the Innu sneaking creature, into the annals of history.

It is a strange looking foot about twelve inches long, narrow at the heel and forking in the front into two broad, round-ended toes. Sometimes its print was so deep that it looked to weigh five hundred pounds ...

So WROTE Elliot Merrick in his book *True North* about a mysterious creature that became known as the Traverspine Gorilla, named after the village it was said to frequent beginning in the autumn of 1913. The story of the so-called gorilla is also covered in a YouTube video as well as in Hynes' *Here Be Dragons*. Besides its very odd tracks—primates do not come with only two toes—the creature also evidenced some very atypical behaviour.

That autumn, a girl with the surname Michelin was playing by herself near the settlement in proximity to her parents' cabin. She spied a strange, manlike being in the woods that was described as having long, dangling arms and a crest of white hair atop its head. That odd mane reminded the witness of the crest on a Roman centurion's helmet. The witness claimed that the creature grinned at her and made hand motions, trying to draw the girl closer.

The child screamed and ran for her cabin, and, upon investigation, the very strange tracks described above were found in the area. Local lumbermen set out to capture or kill the perpetrator, waiting in ambush with their rifles and setting bear traps. The being avoided their machinations, but more tracks were found along with trees stripped of bark and logs that were uprooted.

The "gorilla" stayed around Traverspine for two winters and seemed to have a particular hatred for dogs, harassing them and sometimes even driving them into the local river. Settlers in the area did not appreciate the creature's incursions, as their dogs were often up barking and growling in the night when the "gorilla" was in the area.

The Michelins seemed to be of particular interest to the

creature. In a second sighting at the house, this being was seen looking in a window by one of the children, who, not surprisingly, screamed. The mother was a doughty defender of her brood; the woman charged out the door of the cabin with a shotgun in hand as the creature was disappearing into a clump of willow trees. Mrs. Michelin opened fire into the bush and was rewarded with a meaty thud that indicated she had hit the thing.

When Bruce Wright, a director of the Northeastern Wildlife Station of the University of New Brunswick, spoke with Mrs. Michelin in 1947, he suggested that she had seen a rare barren ground grizzly. Mrs. Michelin scoffed at the idea, stating:

> It was no bear. I have killed twelve myself and I know their tracks well and I saw enough of this thing to be sure of that. I fired a shotgun at it and heard the shot hit. My little girl was playing behind the house and she came running in saying that it was chasing her. I grabbed the shotgun and went outside just in time to get a glimpse of it disappearing in the bush.

As sometimes happens, it seems that Mrs. Michelin either had the two approaches to her children blended together in her mind, or other writers did not have the facts straight about the "gorilla's" approaches to the Michelin home. Regardless, something caused the determined mother to use her shotgun and give us the testimony above. She gave the account of shooting at the creature over thirty years after the event, so we must expect some mixing of stories.

About six months before Wright tried to explain the "gorilla" away, Dr. C. Hogarth Forsyth, the director of a local hospital, spoke about the tracks in a newspaper article. Wright claimed that the tracks were "barefoot" and "ape-like" and that they "sometimes led to nests under the trees". Whatever the track maker was, it cleared obstructions that would have made a human divert from their course. Wright was adamant in stating that the tracks did not belong to a bear since they were seen and identified by trappers who relied on their knowledge of tracks to make a living.

I am convinced that something strange stalked the area of Traverspine during those two winters. Unlike the scientists drenched in their materialist paradigm, if a woman who had personally killed twelve bears and says that she knows their tracks well tells me that what she saw was not a bear, I am going to believe her. The same with trappers who saw tracks they could not explain.

I almost put this story into the section I call Weird Stuff. This creature seems to have been a Sasquatch. Certainly, the fascination with small children and the window peering fit that profile, but this account had two glaringly strange things in it.

First, the tracks were completely atypical for a Sasquatch. Merrick describes them as having two toes. Anyone who has watched a "Bigfoot" documentary knows that the track of a Sasquatch resembles that of a five-toed human only much larger and broader. While there are instances of Sasquatch tracks that appear to have been made by individuals with three or even six toes, five is the most common configuration. If our subject is a primate, then it should have five toes.

Second, the whole business with the creature smiling and gesturing at the Michelin girl is not only superbly creepy but not a typical presentation of Sasquatch behaviour. One wonders if the Travespine Gorilla was not, in fact, a feral human; however, the description of the creature's arms and the weight indicated by the tracks makes this unlikely. Whatever the "gorilla" was, it certainly seemed that it was more than passingly interested in children and willing to try to lure them into the woods. I am reminded of the Albert Ostman story, where a young man is literally carried off by a Sasquatch, and the tales of Native people who believed that Sasquatch sometimes stole children.

All in all, this is an interesting historical account, but, as I could find no modern-day sightings of Sasquatch in Labrador, I am forced to wonder if the First Nations people are not correct, and the creatures are extinct in that area.

NEWFOUNDLAND

Sasquatch also has a historical presence in Newfoundland. In a newspaper article from the *Fort Wayne Daily Gazette*, dated 25 March 1884, we find the following:

> It is reported by a man who lives on one of the spurs on Lookout Mountain that there is a wild man roaming about who is of giant size and as hairy as a Newfoundland dog and as well as he can guess, about nine feet high and will weigh near five hundred pounds—his eyes giving light equal to the moon—an appearance of the most frightful nature and growls equal to a lion, causing the people in that section to remain home of nights with closed doors and well fastened.

This somewhat breathless account certainly seems to describe a Sasquatch though I am curious about the eyes that gave light equivalent to the moon. Did this mean that the eyes were self-illuminating—a sign of a more paranormal creature— or that the settlers had seen bright eye shine in relation to the animal?

Though rare, Sasquatch have also been spotted in Newfoundland in more modern times.

━

WE WILL MEET a Sasquatch sighted along a roadside in Newfoundland in 2008 when we talk about roadside sightings, but Wes Germer, of the *Sasquatch Chronicles* blog, also gives us an interesting Newfoundland sighting from 2012.

Collecting firewood is a seasonal pastime in Canada. Many is the house in the Great White North that has a fireplace or wood-burning stove of some sort. For many, burning wood helps to keep down energy costs in the winter, and there are those for whom wood burning is their primary heat source.

The witness in this case was on his yearly wood collecting trip with three friends. One of the party had a cabin in the forest, and in the winter of 2012, the four had established themselves in the routine of cutting large amounts of firewood and then hauling it back to their homes.

Part of their routine included one of the party rising early, getting the stove going and preparing breakfast. On the morning of the sighting, it was the witness' turn to prepare the morning meal, so he was up before his cohorts. As the bacon was cooking, he put on some warm clothes, as the morning was quite cold, and went outside to "take in the morning air".

As he stood outside, the witness noticed what he thought was a manlike figure leaning against a tree, out in the dense forest. The sun was just coming up, and visibility was poor, so he shrugged the visual impression off, assuming that his eyes were playing tricks on him.

The smell of cooking bacon, as it will, had awakened the rest of the party, and the witness mentioned his odd sighting. The four decided to go back out and have a further look. The sun was up, and visibility had improved, so when they looked off in the indicated direction, all four men saw the figure still motionless against the tree. The witness commented that it was almost as though the manlike subject was asleep, it was so still.

The four men continued their observation:

> We kept our mouths shut and just watched until the sun was fully up. As it kept getting brighter and brighter we were astonished. Leaning against this tree was indeed a man. Well, what we assumed must have been a man ... but ... there was something very very odd. This "man" was jet black from head to toe. We couldn't even make out a face right away it was so black. It was leaning on its right shoulder, with its head leaning to the right ... and what I distinctly remember is that the top of its head was touching a branch. A branch that we figured must have been 7 feet off the ground. We discussed this quietly coming to the conclusion that this had to be a very big tall man wearing some sort of head to toe black suit. We were baffled and couldn't believe what we were seeing. Where did he come from and what was he doing here. Especially that early in the morning.

The four men quickly realized that their attempts to fit this incident into normalcy were in vain. As the sun grew brighter, the party realized that the figure was not wearing black clothing but was covered from head to toe in black fur. With some hesitancy, the witness called out to the figure with no results. Eventually, one of the men picked up two hunks of wood and clacked them together. The resultant noise sounded like a gunshot.

> Immediately this thing's head shot up and looked directly at us. We nearly all fell back. Now we could see that this was definitely not a man. This thing's eyes and teeth were as white as the snow. Well, they appeared to be because the rest of this thing was so black. Its mouth and eyes were so wide I

guess because we had scared the you know what out of it. I'll never forget it. What looked at us that day was more ape than man.

The creature took off into the woods "like a bat out of hell", and the group could hear movement in the trees for ten minutes or so after this.

The entire party was so shaken by this event that the owner of the cabin eventually sold it. The witness stated that he didn't have a good night's sleep for approximately five years after the incident. And, the witness noted, he now simply buys his firewood.

I find this account fascinating. Why on earth would this Sasquatch have fallen asleep against a tree in an area where it had to know that humans were about? The witness noted that, when the animal moved away from the tree, it move awkwardly. Given the almost universal impression of most witnesses that these creatures move very smoothly, one wonders if this specimen was ill or injured in some way.

———

As the reader will have seen over the course of this overview, I was able to find sightings for the Sasquatch or something similar in all the Canadian provinces except Nunavut.

The lack of sightings in Nunavut isn't too surprising when you consider that all the province is in the Arctic climate zone. There is not a lot of cover for a large primate, and the Sasquatch, from some of our witness statements, seems to be an ambush predator. Leaving aside the few outlier prairie sightings, this creature seems to prefer the cover of dense woodland. In addition, Nunavut is sparsely populated, and most of its residents are indigenous people. As I've noted before, the Native peoples are not as quick to talk about Sasquatch as other people might be.

Now that we have established that the Sasquatch is seen all throughout Canada, I want to focus on a peculiarity of the Sasquatch that I think doesn't get mentioned enough and that seems to me to be a first indication that this creature may not be at all what it seems.

CHAPTER SIX
WHY DID THE SASQUATCH CROSS THE ROAD?

WHEN READING through the stories of Sasquatch encounters (and, for that matter, many cryptid sightings), we quickly see that these creatures are often sighted near or in the process of crossing roads. I had not really thought about this until I did the research for my book *Phantom Black Dogs: Walkers of the Liminal Ways*. Please indulge me while I quote from my own text:

> The Phantom Black Dog takes this obsession with roads a step farther. While you might expect a dog-like entity from the Otherworld to run wild on the moors of England, the lore shows that you are far more likely to run into our subject on a roadside, coming out of a hedge.

In *Phantom Black Dogs*, I lay out a theory of the Black Dog apparition using ley lines as energy sources for their appearance, but I won't belabour that point. Instead, it seems to me that the Sasquatch and other cryptids may be influenced by another aspect of roads—the fact that they are, by their nature, liminal areas.

In faery lore, such spots are referred to as betwixt and between. A road is neither this place, nor that place; it is a transit point between the places. Because of that liminal nature, streets, roads, and highways are areas where the Veil Between the Worlds can be thin, and any number of interesting things may occur.

I am going to lay out some of the many roadside sightings I discovered in my research in this section and then give some thoughts on why I think that the Sasquatch is seen so often along roads, trails, and other places of human travel. For a creature that is supposed to be so elusive, the Sasquatch has managed to make itself known along travel routes in every province I've noted previously.

———

BEGINNING IN ALBERTA, we have this brief roadside encounter from the sighting database at *Alberta Sasquatch*, report #065.

This happened years ago!! I was driving a gravel truck out past the Suncor gas plant down the Simonette road. It was an awesome clear summer day, I had just crossed shell creek and started up the hill, at the top of [the] hill the road turns to the left with cut lines on both sides. As I crested the hill I noticed something big and dark run up on the road, at first thought [it] was a bear, but as I got closer it got bigger, it took off across the road upright and went down the cut line, never once did it drop on all fours, I stopped at [the] cut line and no sign of it. I had co-workers come to the spot and help me look for tracks but the muskeg on the cut line was spongy and just popped up and as for the road it was packed solid from all the oilfield traffic so nothing there. No way it was a bear, I'm thinking at least 8 feet tall and it's something I'll never forget.

I've entitled this section "Why Did the Sasquatch Cross the Road?" for a reason. In many of these encounters, not only does a driver and/or passengers spot a Sasquatch, but the creature then proceeds to cross the road, usually in front of the vehicle.

In another report, #041, from *Alberta Sasquatch*, we see a reaction to the sighting that is very commonplace:

It was the last week of May 2004 on the Akamina Parkway in Waterton National Park. Early in the morning ... it was overcast, light drizzle. I was driving and remember thinking to myself that there were a lot of Snowshoe Hare along side the road eating the fresh greens. I focused on one Hare on the left side of the parkway, but my attention quickly focused on [the] right side of the road and saw a large black figure looking at the Hare and then quickly looking at me. It was standing in the ditch and with its left arm turned away a branch as if to get a better look at me then as quickly as it happened it ended. I kept driving past wondering to myself what I had just seen. I was in a daze of sorts, trying to comprehend what I just saw. I did not stop to try and get a picture nor did I stop to look for prints. I was just in a mild state of shock ...

Despite the brevity of the sighting, this witness notes, in further thoughts around the incident, that they still think of the sighting, even though the event occurred in 2004 or 2005 and was reported to the website in 2018. The sighting of a Sasquatch (or other cryptid) often burns itself into the witness' memory and can be recalled with clarity years later.

I would also note that this sighting occurred near Waterton Lakes National Park, the site of two encounters that I noted earlier, including the well-documented Crandell Lake campground incident.

BFRO report #65338, gives the very detailed sighting of Liz Manley, an emergency medical responder for an oilfield about seventy kilometres south of Grand Prairie. The event occurred in 2004 as Manley was travelling an oilfield service road.

The site was closing down due to the spring break-up, a period of melting snow and ice that turns the ground into sludge. Manley was the last to exit the site, following a truck with tie-down issues that departed the area at about 0330 hours. The medical responder waited about twenty minutes to allow that vehicle to get far enough ahead of her that her medical unit would not be peppered with debris thrown up by the larger truck.

Finally departing at around 0400 hours, Manley had been on duty since 0700 the previous morning. As she was going into her twenty-first hour on duty, she was being very attentive to both sides of the service road and maintaining a speed of thirty to forty kilometres per hour (between nineteen and twenty-four miles per hour). Wildlife encounters were common in the area, and Manley reported that she had seen deer, elk, lynx, moose, black bears and even a grizzly sow during her time at the site.

Manley kept the high beams of the mobile treatment centre (MTC) that she was driving on, and those lights were illuminating the entire roadbed as well as snow and ice piled along the edge of the road and ten metres to each side of the road. In addition, because of the snow left on the ground, Manley could make out details out past her lights.

The witness noted that, at five feet two inches, if the road grades were very steep, she had difficulty seeing the road ahead of her. Given the steep grading of some parts of the road she was travelling, Manley had slowed down to twenty kilometres per hour (a little over twelve miles per hour) and was glad that she had. An elk stepped out from the right side of the road, leapt the berm, and stopped in the middle of the road.

Narrowly avoiding the animal, Manley took stock of the elk, noting that it had been running hard and had its nose in the air as if it wanted to bugle. The elk's tongue was hanging from its mouth, and its eyes were rolled back such that the sclera were exposed. It was not rutting season, and Manley could think of no reason why the creature would be so distressed.

After standing for several seconds, the elk dropped its head into a more normal position and continued its progress off the left side of the road. The witness, experienced in the ways of elk and deer, knew that if there was one elk, there might be others about to cross. She cast her eyes down both sides of the road, looking for eye shine, before she was prepared to drive on.

Manley stated that normal procedure was for gas field roads to be clear cut along the right side to allow for pipe to be laid to pump the gas out. The pipeline had not been laid for this road, so tree stumps were still in evidence. Manley had finished her cautious check of the area and was about to get moving again when she saw movement in her peripheral vision.

Initially, the witness thought she was looking at a tree stump a little taller than those that surrounded it. She was soon disabused of this notion:

A slight breeze moved the fur/hair of this taller stump and it sort of shimmered like the hollow tips on a grizzly's coat in the trucks [sic] head lights. Looking closer, I now see what appears to be a round head, no face visible, and two round shoulders. The width outside shoulder to outside shoulder had to be at least three football helmets wide, at least 1 meter. The bulkiness of the shoulders should have been another clue that the shape of this form was not that of a bear. This [was] my "Aha!" moment and I am now thinking I now know what was making the elk run; a bear and by its colouring a Grizzly. I feel the puzzle has been solved satisfactorily and start to move forward; that's when it stands up on two legs!

When I say it stands, what it does is it unfolds in a smooth and easy motion, no swaying, no side to side in the way a bear does to keep in a standing position. I am still thinking grizzly bear. Based on its estimated distance from the side of the road, about 10–12m, the brightness of the area being lit by the high beams and how the upper part of the standing form fades into darkness, I would guesstimate the height to be 7 to 8 feet.

The creature turned its upper body to the east, but the witness was unable to get a good look at the face, as the upper third of the creature faded into the darkness. Nevertheless, Manley had the notion that this being was looking farther down the road that she was travelling.

Manley was completely dissuaded from thinking the animal was a bear when its arms dropped into place. She reported that she could see "the range of motion, shape and the large shape of a hand in the light of the high beams". She also noted that the arm came to a place lower than it would have been on a human.

As so often happens in these cases, the medic was overcome with the feeling that she really needed to begin moving away from the creature. Manley likened this to a compulsion and said that her heart was beating fast, and her hair was standing up as she put the MTC in motion. Once she had recovered from the shock of the sighting, the witness quickly concluded that she had seen a Sasquatch.

These three examples from Alberta are but three of many from across Canada. Let's look now at some roadside encounters from Manitoba.

━━

HIGHWAY 6 in Manitoba and its surrounds seem to be a common ground for Sasquatch sightings. Here is a roadside sighting that happened along that highway taken from the BFRO database (report #12335) and edited slightly for spelling:

> I was proceeding north, late afternoon, first Monday in September 1990. Traffic was light. I had just passed Devils Lake roadside park. A compact pickup truck with two occupants (male and female) passed me, and was 200 yards in front of me. Visibility was good, in full sun. The road has wide ditches with scrub on the right (east) and spruce forest 40 yards from the road on the left (west). The foliage in the ditch was brown and past ripe. I was watching the truck in front of me proceed away from me as I maintained a constant speed of approximately 110 km per h when something that had been lying in the ditch, blending in very well, rose to a height exceeding 7 feet and proceeded across the road, from right to left, and into the bush. The individual was about midway between me and the next truck. It was very very quick, did not look at me. It was looking straight ahead, instead. It had long legs, bent at the knee, a large chest, long arms, and a round head. I think the face was dark brown, and the body hair was roughly the colour of coconut husk. I proceeded to the Easterville corner, and phoned home to tell my wife what I had seen.

A couple of interesting notes about this sighting. First, we see a Sasquatch trait that is mentioned frequently in sightings. This creature paid no attention at all to the oncoming car. It simply went about its business as though walking in front of a vehicle moving at one hundred ten kilometres per hour (about sixty-eight miles per hour) was an everyday occurrence.

The other item of interest is emphasized throughout the sightings in this book. The witness noted that the animal was "very, very quick". Whether it is scaling hillsides, jumping from one place to another, or ambushing a deer, witnesses testify to the speed and grace of these creatures, often attributing almost supernatural physical attributes to the animal. The Special Forces soldier who reported sighting a Sasquatch bagging a deer likened its speed to that of a cheetah!

That is quite an accomplishment for an animal that is reportedly eight or more feet tall and very heavy as well.

Another Manitoba roadside sighting gives us another feature of the animal that is often noted. This sighting came from witness "DJ", and I quote the BFRO database (report #1281). Again, the account is slightly edited for spelling.

> I was the driver of the vehicle and my cousin was the passenger. I was driving down highway #6 just nearing the bridge named "North Three Rivers Creek Bridge", when all of a sudden what I thought was a man came out of the left side of the bush. I immediately awoke my cousin and told her to take a look at this guy, the very first thing I noticed was what I thought were his clothing (black) and his "walk", both being out of the norm. I thought that this guy might not be all there, his walk looked as though he was marching. He made his way down the ditch and onto the highway and at that moment I without a doubt thought it looked like a Bigfoot. His walk was so distinct, it took amazing strides with his arms swinging. It was covered head to toe in black fur and appeared to be without a neck. I was expecting it to look in my direction, but it just kept walking, heading towards the other side of the highway. As I was nearing, it made its way onto the right side

of the highway, the ditch. As I was passing it, it made its way in to the bush. I braked, but could not see it for the bush was thick. I was not going to get out and start exploring because I was quite shaken from the whole ordeal. So, I continued down the highway. In the five-hour drive, not once could I stop thinking about what happened.

Once again, we see the detail of the animal completely ignoring the vehicle and going about its business. Here, too, is a terrific example of something that people often note in Sasquatch sightings—the creature's unusual gait.

As you look through the reports in this book, you will see, time and time again, words along the line of, "it wasn't a bear ..." followed by some notation about the way the animal moved. The creature is often noted to have been completely bipedal and to walk with a long-legged gait that covers an inordinate amount of ground in a short period of time. The Sasquatch is often seen to traverse distances that human witnesses later took much longer to negotiate, and it seems to do this with ease.

I am minded of the words of witness Claire, from the famous *Sasquatch Chronicles* podcast episode 515, in which she described the movement of the creatures she saw by saying that they almost seemed to glide along a California beach where she was taking photos. She, too, noted that she knew what a bear looked like and that there was "no way that what I saw were bears".

The Sasquatch is also seen on roadsides in Ontario.

MARKDALE, Ontario, was the site of a 1964 road sighting that features an unusual aspect. The witness, reporting to the BFRO in report #31992, was in his early teens, riding with his parents in the family car at night. The witness was sitting in the back seat and gazing out the right rear window of the vehicle when he noted "standing up on the embankment at the tree-line a tall fur covered creature".

The witness noted that the embankment in question rose almost ten feet along the side of the road. Naturally, after spotting the animal, the witness turned to look out the rear window of the car. The creature was clearly visible in the brake lights of the car as the driver slowed for a stop sign. There was also light from a "lodge across the road", and the witness observed the creature from distances of thirty-five feet to three hundred feet as the car moved.

As often happens with young witnesses, when the teen tried to turn his parents' attention to the subject, they ignored him and drove on. The witness is convinced he saw a Sasquatch since "no bear walks down an embankment on its hind legs". The witness also ruled out a hoax because of the size of the creature and the effort it took not to be seen.

I found this incident interesting since the Sasquatch passed behind the car. So often, in roadside encounters, the creature blithely walks along the side of the road or crosses in front of the encroaching car. One wonders, after reading this account, how many of these animals might be sighted if more vehicles had passengers looking out the back window?

The reader may recall that one set of sightings that is often mentioned in Sasquatch books are the ones for Old Yellowtop, a Sasquatch that seemingly made itself a part of the history of Cobalt, Ontario, for decades. This being was not the only Sasquatch sighted in that area, as this roadside event, recorded in BFRO report #16807 will demonstrate. Again, the account has been edited slightly for typos.

Driving southbound on a fairly busy road looking at the scenery and just noticing a large black movement to the right. Initially I thought a black burnt-out tree trunk but the arm swing was the giveaway. I noticed the movement of the arms in a full motion from front to back. It only lasted about 6 seconds but as I couldn't see it anymore—due to my wife's head in the way. Sounds funny but seconds later as the sighting was sinking in and my mind was trying to figure out what I just saw, my wife said, "I just saw a Sasquatch." I immediately stopped and turned around but there was no further sighting.

She said that it looked like a moss man. All clumpy blackish hair with no neck. She only saw it from the waist up also. All we kept saying is how unreal it was to see and how big it was. The arms were massive.

In this account, we see another aspect of these sightings that is often mentioned by witnesses—arm swing. I mentioned in the previous section that the Sasquatch seems to have a very distinctive gait, one that separates it clearly from a bear walking briefly on its hind legs, and part of that gait is the evident arm swing.

We see this feature clearly in the renowned Patterson-Gimlin film (available on multiple sites on the internet), where the subject is taking the characteristic long strides of a Sasquatch as well as moving her arms in a wide swing, back and forth, as she walks. The smooth walk demonstrated in the film and attested to by many witnesses, coupled with the arm swing, are not evident in bears walking on their hind legs.

In BFRO report #1291, we encounter another aspect of Sasquatch behaviour that has been noted by other researchers. The incident occurred in June of 1993 on McLeod Road in Renfrew County. Incidentally, this area is not far from Algonquin Provincial Park, an area that has a fair number of Sasquatch sightings.

The witness, Desmond Warren, and his girlfriend of the time had chosen to park along McLeod Road, a "gravel back-road that parallels the south shore of the Madawaska River". The couple had left a party in the early morning hours and had backed into the entrance to an old logging trail. Both parties noted an odour in the area "like a sewer backed up, or rotten meat", but this smell did not, apparently, dissuade them.

Sometime between 0530 and 0600 hours, the witness exited the vehicle to urinate. As he stood at the rear of the car, he heard a noise to his left and turned to see a "large, black, hairy creature standing upright only 30 feet from him". Warren had no doubt what he was seeing, as the animal stood motion-less, watching him as he made his way back to the car, finishing his business along the way.

The witness, unlike a lot of Sasquatch experiencers, urged his girlfriend to get out of the car so that she could see the crea-ture too. The report is not clear about whether the young lady exited the vehicle but does note that she, too, saw the Sasquatch. The animal, noting this observation, took ten or fifteen strides to get back into the forest cover and, after watching the two for a few moments longer, moved away from the scene. Warren noted the arm swing of the creature as it moved, a characteristic we have noted previously.

Warren and the female witness then departed the scene, "shaken and stunned". Warren gave a very detailed description of the Sasquatch:

> I'm 5'11", and it was a good two feet taller than me. It was at least 3' wide. It was completely covered with long blackish brown hair, from its head right down to its toes. The only places I noticed where there was no hair was around the eyes

and the hands. I could see that in the chest area—there was less hair in there, like on a gorilla. It had a chest like a body builder. The hair went right down its arms almost to the ends of its fingers. On its legs the hair went right down onto its feet. It had big human looking feet. There wasn't much hair on its feet and it had blackish gray toenails—that's how close I was! When it walked away I could see the soles of its feet. They were blackish in colour and very wide—about 6" wide and maybe 14" or 15" long. It was more of a flat foot. The arms were maybe the same length as a mans [sic] but very muscular. It had pretty straight sides, no curves, you know, like on a woman. It had a tall head and not too much of a neck. It had deep sunk eyes and you could see the skin in there, kinda a brownish black leathery look to it. Where we would have eyebrows it had a ridge that stuck out a fair piece. I don't remember anything specific about the mouth, but the nose—two large nostrils like a gorilla. There was hair on the face, but you could make out where the nose area would be.

These details indicate how close the witness was to the creature, but another aspect of the case caught my attention. The witnesses were engaged in the age-old custom of "parking" in a deserted area, presumably to have some alone and perhaps intimate time with his female companion. Warren and his girlfriend are not the first "parkers" to have encountered a Sasquatch, and one wonders what it is about human mating customs that attracts the creature.

Be that as it may, we have still more roadside encounters to peruse. Let's look at a Sasquatch seen on roads in Saskatchewan.

THE WITNESS and family in this case, BFRO report #14405, were driving from Green Lake to Big River when they had their encounter. At 1220 hours on 14 April 2006, the witnesses were travelling on Highway 155 about fifteen kilometres south of Green Lake.

As their vehicle rounded a bend in the road, they observed a green Dodge Caravan approaching from the other direction. They also noted what appeared to be a person urinating in the ditch on the right side of the highway. Amusingly, the BFRO investigator, Blaine McMillan, noted that this was a common practice in the area. I expect that one could say that roadside stops are common along any long stretch of highway with no rest stops!

The witness soon began to doubt the initial impression that he was seeing a human. The "person" seemed to be inordinately tall, and when it moved, it crossed a thirty-foot-wide ditch in four or five strides. The creature walked with the often-noted fluid stride and disappeared quickly into the brush by the time the witness' vehicle came to the spot where the animal had been seen.

The witness also stated that the creature's head had the characteristic conical shape. In addition, no neck was noted; the animal's head seemed to sit directly on it shoulders. McMillan noted that the witness was so impressed by the sighting that he determined that he would carry a camera in his vehicle from then on—just in case.

While this sighting report is not very detailed, it is very typical of the quick, "wait, was that a Sasquatch" encounters that we see so often in this research. Let's take some time now to look to the Yukon and experiences along roads of that province.

SASQUATCH CANADA

I noted the roadside sighting of a family near Craven, Saskatchewan, and the sighting of Shaylane Beatty near Deschambault Lake in that same province. Both road encounters are documented earlier in the book, so I am going to move on to Whitehorse, in the Yukon province, and a 2004 article from the CBS News website.

> It was big and hairy, but it wasn't a bear. Marion Sheldon and Gus Jules are convinced they saw Big Foot along the Alaska Highway near Whitehorse, Yukon. The men say at first they thought they saw a man standing by the side of the road. They turned their all-terrain vehicles around, thinking it was someone who needed a ride. But as the men approached, they say the creature crossed the road in a couple of big steps and went into the bush. Conservation officer Dave Bakica heard their story—and says whatever it was, it shook up the two men. Bakica doesn't know if it was the legendary Sasquatch. But he says by the time he got to the sire [*sic*], any evidence like footprints was gone.

An article from the Associated Press, cited on the BFRO site, gives us further information. Interestingly, the witnesses were both from Teslin, a Tlingit settlement that was experiencing Sasquatch sightings at almost the same time that this event occurred. The article also indicates that the two men got within twenty feet of this creature.

Both Sheldon and Jules were also noted as members of the Tlingit Council in Teslin, and Jules was an experienced hunter. He estimated the height of the creature at about seven feet but stated that it was hunched over. The Sasquatch was described as covered in hair but with some skin showing through.

The conservation officer noted that "ground conditions mixed with rainfall made it impossible to pick up definitive tracks and there was no hair on branches or other vegetation". To make tracking even more difficult, by the time the officer got to the scene, some time later, half the village had been out to the site.

As an end note, the AP reporter stated that there had been another sighting in the Yukon and gave a brief summary of three Pelly Crossing residents who spied a Sasquatch while driving from Pelly to Stewart Crossing. The animal moved back into the woods as the witnesses' vehicle passed, but they took a photo of footprints that appeared to be fifteen inches long. Unfortunately, the prints were in melting snow, a tracking medium that is notorious for misshaping tracks.

Interestingly, for those who have read my book *Canadian Monsters and Mysteries*, the Pelly area was also the site of a large-scale UFO incursion in 1996.

In another Yukon road encounter, witness Peter Stone, a member of the Kaska tribal council, wrote his experience in a letter to the Whitehorse *Daily Star* after seeing derogatory coverage of a Sasquatch sighting on local television. Stone reported that he saw the creature, which his people call Gah Gunna (bushman), about three miles north of the Upper Liard community along the Alaska Highway.

Stone reported that conditions were clear with no snow on the ground and "near warm" temperatures. It was dusk, so the witness still had light to see by. He was approaching a light green minivan, and both vehicles were travelling south. Rather than pass, Stone reduced speed and followed the other vehicle at a distance. The drive was uneventful until Stone rounded a corner on a downhill stretch of road and noticed that the minivan had slowed.

As he slowed down, the witness noted a flash of "shadow movement" to the right of the lead vehicle and assumed that it was a moose. Apparently, this sighting took place late in the moose rutting season. As might be expected, if one sighted a moose, the minivan braked suddenly and veered off to the right, coming to a stop on the gravel shoulder of the road. Stone had some concern that the maneuver might take the vehicle over the low road-bank.

"A dark form moved in a fluid motion across the roadway to the left shoulder." Stone was faced with two concerns: determining if there had been any injuries in the near crash and seeing what had crossed the road in front of him and the hapless minivan. He reported slowing down and moving toward the centre of the road as he approached the stopped vehicle.

The witness was about thirty feet from the near-accident site when he looked to his left and spied the Sasquatch. "Time stood still, my expression was awe and is this real! ... Unexplainable is the strange realization I had of being in a slow-motion movie where there was no sound but realism." In what the witness described as a "surreal trance", the man recalled words from his father, chose not to panic and decided that he needed to remember all that he could, as this would likely be the only time he would see such a creature.

Stone described Gah Gunna as seven plus feet tall. The body was covered in grey fur "with a dirt brown tinge of short hair". The witness noted no shaggy or long strands of hair but stated that there was a "bald area between the cheekbone and nose ..." The nose was not clearly visible, as he was looking at the creature face on, but he testified that the being was upright, not slouched, and that its arms hung to the sides.

The head struck the witness as more humanlike, and while its shoulders were broad and appeared strong, the creature was "tall, big-boned, lean with muscle and a neck that [was] neither short nor long. The hands were big, with its fingers noticeably set apart. Ears [were] small and close to the head".

Upon making eye contact with the Sasquatch, Stone was

convinced of the creature's human-level intellect. He had the clear impression of the being as assessing the situation and being wary rather than predatory or frightened. The animal disappeared into the bush, and Stone moved past the minivan, which had backed out onto the road, and went on his way when he realized that the other vehicle was driving back north. He surmised that the van's occupants were headed off in the opposite direction to report the incident.

We have established that the Sasquatch likes to cross roads up north; let's look east now.

In July of 2002, BFRO report #15343 gives us yet another example of a road sighting. The witness, who lived in Arizona, was driving on New Brunswick Route 4, returning from his daughter's wedding in Canada. The witness was driving while his wife rested her eyes, and they were not far from the Canada-Maine border somewhere between the towns of McAdam and Yorks Mill.

The driver was in a very isolated area, and when he spotted a maroon Oldsmobile parked along the side of the road, with no one in evidence around it, he watched it closely, fearing the possibility of a hold-up. The stopped car had his attention until he glanced up at the highway and spied a Sasquatch in the middle of the road, in the process of crossing.

The creature was "well-built" without much body fat with hair/fur that seemed neat but that did not appear to be dense. The witness stated that he could see dark skin through the hair that covered the animal. As they are so often described, the Sasquatch did not appear to have a neck, and the animal was looking down, so the driver could discern no facial features.

The witness described seeing the creature's leg muscles

bunch and release as it made its way across the road and across the ditch at the roadside. At no time did the Sasquatch appear to break stride; its gait was smooth, not breaking stride even when it came to the ditch.

Interestingly, the witness was so shocked by what he had seen that he did not think to wake his wife. She only learned of the event after the sighting was over.

BFRO investigator Todd Prescott noted that the witness thought that he was the victim of a prank at first (although why someone would do this on an isolated road in New Brunswick is anyone's guess). As so often happens with Sasquatch witnesses, this driver tried to fit what he was seeing into something he could explain and failed utterly. Prescott reported that the longer the witness watched the animal, the more convinced he became, because of its unusual gait, that the animal was not human, or a human dressed in a suit.

In another sighting, in 2006, BFRO report #17221 details a typical road encounter but with an amusing ending.

> My wife and I were driving from Moncton to Sackville on New Brunswick #2 in June 2006 in the afternoon and saw a figure walking across a clearing about a 100 yards away. It was all black, walked with long strides and arms out and we did not see any clothes such as a shirt or blue jeans. We could not see any facial features. It was about 4 to 5 PM. We tell our friends that since my wife and I seldom agree on anything, but do on this, it had to be Bigfoot.

I appreciated the witness' honesty in saying that it had to be a Sasquatch since both he and his wife agreed on what they had seen. Apparently, the couple found their agreement unusual enough to mention.

Todd Prescott also investigated this case and spoke to the

couple for further details. The man, who was driving at the time, had to focus on driving and so had fewer details to share. The creature was dark in colour, somewhere between six and seven feet tall and walking in a casual manner with no hint of stress or worry about the vehicle.

The wife, who was not driving and could pay closer attention, agreed with her husband that the being was covered in dark hair and approximately six to seven feet tall. She additionally noted that the "creature 'lumbered' along bipedally with an unusual, non-human gait (that is, its arms seemed proportionally longer than the typical arm/torso ratio as seen in humans, and it appeared to take long strides)".

I also found a YouTube video about this sighting titled "New Brunswick, Canada Bigfoot Sighting", and picked up a couple of additional details. The range of the sighting was about seventy to eighty yards, and the creature stayed in the field on the left-hand side of the road. There was no attempt to cross the road, but the witnesses both agreed that they thought the being was moving from one sector of dense mixed woods to another.

Let's move our roadside survey to the province of Quebec now.

SIGHTINGS FROM QUEBEC, for whatever reason, are not thick on the ground. The following account, from witness Roger Couture, was reported on the *Sasquatch Canada* website. The event occurred 12 February 2009 on Road 109, which runs north to south between Matagami and Amos.

The witness had been on a successful elk hunt and was on his way back to his home in a medium-sized city east of Montreal. He left Matagami at about 0815 hours and was proceeding along the 109 at about ninety kilometres per hour (about fifty-six miles per hour) on that clear, cold February day. There was considerable forest cover with mixed fir, spruce, poplar, and birch.

At about 0910, Couture came to a straight stretch of road that gave him a view for a considerable distance ahead. The witness spied what he at first thought was a large, black garbage container on the side of the road at a range of 400 to 450 metres (437 to 492 yards). He found this strange, as there were no dwellings in the area.

As Couture got closer, he found that the subject was walking toward him, down the hill, on the shoulder of the road. Once he had disabused himself of the notion that he was seeing a garbage bin, he then moved to the idea that this was a tall person dressed in what might be a black snowmobile suit with a hood. In this way, the witness sought to explain the uniformity of colour that he was seeing with the subject. A hood helped him explain the bell shape of the subject's head.

Couture goes on to detail his observations about the creature:

- the being did not seem to reflect light and was a uniform colour all over
- the bodily proportions could have been those of a human in a snowsuit
- clear movement of the legs was noted with legs of a uniform diameter from waist to feet
- movement of the head as it walked suggested that the creature was taking long strides
- the arms did not move, as the being seemed to be holding something in front of it; the elbows were at ninety degrees
- the shoulders were broad with a slight angle

- the head was bell-shaped, but Couture could see a lighter vertical line on the face that indicated a nose to him
- the witness had the impression that the creature was easily overtopping the three-foot snowbanks

Interestingly, what convinced the witness that he had seen a Sasquatch was not his observations but the disappearance of the animal. Couture glanced in his rear-view mirror when another vehicle topped the rise, and when he looked back, the subject was gone. Couture calculated that the creature would have had to clear twenty feet of snow in order to disappear into the trees.

When the witness went back to look at the site, the snow in that area proved to be quite treacherous and hard to negotiate, yet the creature had managed it in the time it took the witness to look in his rear-view mirror and then back to the road. Couture was puzzled by this vanishing act and conjectured that the creature had jumped the distance when he was unable to find tracks. We will look at another two cases of disappearing Sasquatch in a later section of the book.

———

I WILL CONCLUDE the sightings for this section with one from Lon Strickler's *Phantoms and Monsters* blog. In about 2008, the witness, identified as John, was en route to the town of Branch with a friend. The two were travelling to retrieve a car that the friend's uncle was fixing up. The duo successfully picked up the vehicle and were driving back, cautiously watching for moose, as it was an hour or two before sunset, prime moose-movement time.

As anyone who has lived in Canada for more than a few minutes will tell you, a car versus moose accident is one to be avoided at all costs. According to Canada's Traffic Injury Research Foundation, 236 people died in collisions with Canadian moose in the time from 2000 to 2014. The gangly animals are so tall that they are known to completely take the top off vehicles in an accident, so John's diligence in watching for moose was quite intelligent.

The two were following the vehicle they had gone to recover, driven by a person identified only as D. D had his headlights on bright, and as almost expected, a moose calf and its mother wandered onto the road. The two cars slowed, and John indicated that the group was watching the tree line closely, looking for other moose.

They did not see another moose but instead had the following encounter:

> ... in the ditch, on the left side of the road is a giant human-shaped hairy ape. We all saw it when D's headlights lit him up and as our tail-lights hit him, he was doing that turning back look from the Patterson Film. The damn thing was eye level with me sitting in the car and it was standing in the ditch staring at me with dark green eyes from the reflection and without pause it took two strides out of the ditch into the woods. None of us had cellphones so we planned to stop at an old train bridge over an old water fall and when we pulled up beside D's car and rolled down the window, D leaned over and said, Did you guys see the hairy naked man in the ditch? We were speechless and no one wanted to get out of the car so we just got back on the road and left. Yes, we have bears and I have seen bears stumble on hind legs but this was no bear. This was Bigfoot!

Again, note the long stride of these creatures—"two strides out of the ditch into the woods"—and the fact that, even after they had travelled some distance from the site of the event, none of these gentlemen wanted to get out of their cars!

Sasquatch definitely makes an impression on people.

As we have seen, Sasquatch and roads seem to go together no matter what Canadian province we visit. As I mentioned in the first section of this chapter, there are many road encounters that I could not include here because of space considerations.

But why is it that the Sasquatch seems to favour roads almost as much as the Phantom Black Dog apparition? One of the ideas that has been set forth about Sasquatch is that the creature is either a relict hominid or, possibly, an undiscovered species of great ape indigenous to North America. One common theory is that *Gigantopithecus blacki,* a species of giant ape in the hominid family, migrated over the Bering Sea land bridge thousands of years ago and established a home territory here in North America.

While this theory has its proponents and detractors, I am not going to get into the arguments pro and con. Rather, I am going to use this idea as a focus for my thoughts on this issue.

Let's say, for the sake of argument, that such a migration did occur and that these giant apes were now native to North America. Forget for a moment that Sasquatch-like creatures are reported all over the globe; let us simply focus on our North American backyard.

It seems obvious in the extreme, but such a creature, in order to survive the continuing encroachment of humans on its habitat, would have to be a master of camouflage. There is a good reason why there are T-shirts extant with stylized pictures of Sasquatch proclaiming the creature the hide-and-seek champion of the world! Despite the best efforts of Sasquatch hunters all over Canada and the United States, the Hairy One continues to be elusive, yielding plenty of circumstantial and anecdotal evidence for its existence but nothing rising to the level of scientific proof.

Now, part of this problem may be the stubborn resistance of science to actually do science and fund investigation into the creature. My point, though, is that the Sasquatch is an extremely elusive creature.

I think that most Sasquatch researchers would say that the subject of their quest is hard to find for a reason. It recognizes, as do most wild animals, that humans are not its friends. If the species has been extant on this continent for thousands of years, as indigenous lore seems to assert, then it has watched as humans have torn up progressively more and more of its habitat. It would seem to me that these depredations combined with the presence of hunters with their weapons would drive the Sasquatch deeper into the forest and make them very chary of contact with humankind.

Instead, we find them repeatedly being sighted on the sides of roads or even crossing roads, and they are sometimes seen to do this in overtly populated areas. A September 1997 sighting (BFRO report #1340) saw two truck drivers spotting a Sasquatch under a bridge on Highway 406 in St. Catharines, Ontario (slight spelling and punctuation correction).

> Bulky Hairy (Brown Hair) being walking under the bridge. We are Tractor Trailer Drivers and both saw a Bigfoot Sept. 3, 1997 3:00PM Central Time. Hwy. 406 ... We were crossing a bridge (westbound) that has solid cement rails all the way across. Cars have no way of seeing over the rails down the 100 feet or so to the bottom. This is where we seen the big hairy creature walking south on the west bank. Well, when I pointed for Margie (passenger seat) to see as we were

going by at around 50–60 mph, she seen the creature going north in the same location. The water beside the creature looked about ankle deep, pouring south. The creature was on the rocky part (dry). The creature was looking straight ahead (south) and to the side (east) towards the water. Walking along as we would walk to town or something. The creature was completely full of hair. I do remember seeing some flesh on the arms and elbows. The feet and ankles were massive. The ankles were as massive as the legs. The long hair looked groomed all over the body too (brownish hair). Also the arms appeared to be longer than usual. That was what caused my first real attention to it.

I found this sighting to be, frankly, astonishing. These truckers saw a Sasquatch under a bridge in a city of over 115,000 people adjacent to a busy highway. To add to all this, the sighting occurred in broad daylight!

It is true that wildlife does use creek and riverbeds to move about in the urban areas of Canada. I have several such natural thoroughfares near my home in Kitchener and have seen coyotes, foxes, skunks, raccoons and other creatures on my daily walks. I've also heard howling in the night that was most likely coyotes down in the creek beds near me.

Now, I suppose it is possible that the Sasquatch, too, are simply following prey down into populated areas. I've not seen them, but I have been told by locals that there are deer down in the creek and riverbeds I mentioned. We've seen a Sasquatch taking a deer in one of the earlier witness stories, and there are plenty of US accounts that seem to indicate that ungulates make up some portion of the Sasquatch's diet.

Still, given the number of times that we have seen these creatures encounter a human only to turn and disappear into the forest, I find it hard to believe that an animal that shy of human contact would venture into a city. This is also why I wonder about roadside encounters.

Most researchers seem to feel that the Sasquatch has better than human senses of hearing and smell and perhaps even sight. While it may be that the creature wanders in search of food, if the Sasquatch is as cautious of people as it seems to be, then why is it seen near roads so often? If, as many researchers assert, these beings are highly intelligent, then why would they not simply take alternate routes and avoid roads altogether? And, if they found that they must cross a road, why would they not bide their time and cross when they would not be seen? Why, instead, would the creature step out in front of an oncoming vehicle, often one coming at a high rate of speed? And why on earth would the animal seem almost detached as it performed this high-risk maneuver?

Witness after witness reports that, not only do Sasquatch cross roads but that they seem to not even be paying attention when they do so. While some witnesses report creatures turning and looking at them, many state that the creature went about its business **as if they were not there**.

I think this last might be the key to an idea that I am going to explore in the final sections of this book. We've seen that people are definitely having the experience of something out in the forests and along roadsides that looks like a giant, bipedal ape, or hominid. My feeling is that, as we go deeper into the background of the Sasquatch, we will begin to see that there is something strange that lurks around the Sasquatch phenomenon.

I am going to start my examination of this topic by exploring some sightings that don't fit into the hypothesis that Sasquatch is a flesh and blood creature.

CHAPTER SEVEN
STRANGE THINGS

TIMOTHY RENNER AND JOSHUA CUTCHIN, in their book series *Where the Footprints End*, do an admirable job of covering many aspects of the strange surrounding the Sasquatch phenomenon. Unfortunately for my purposes, most of their data comes from the United States, but I will be referring to their books more than once in this section.

In an interesting historical note, Renner and Cutchin briefly recount the tale of the Waterdown "Ghost".

Most of us, when we think of ghosts, think of shades of a deceased human. In Watertown, a small community in Ontario that is now part of the city of Hamilton, the ghost of something that appeared to be a gorilla manifested several times in the summer of 1934. The "gorilla ghost" allegedly sent some of the women in a group of picnickers into "hysterics" when it appeared in the light of fires built to roast corn.

We aren't given any description of the "ghost" other than that it was hairy, but the gorilla description must put us in mind of the subject of this book. One wonders, in considering this brief account, why the citizens of Watertown viewed these sightings as apparitional rather than as that of a physical creature.

It is certainly the case that Sasquatch is known for its stealth, and these cases may simply be an example of the creatures coming close to civilization, for reasons of their own, but questions remain:

1. Why would these shy, elusive creatures make themselves so plainly known?
2. Why would the people who saw them assume them to be ghosts?
3. If they were actually ghosts, then what were they the spirits of?

Most curious and a good start to a section that will leave the reader with more questions than answers.

IN HIS BOOK on strange creatures of Newfoundland and Labrador, Bruce Hynes relates a story from folklore researcher Michael Taft.

An uncorroborated tale is told of a Battle Point bootlegger who buried his illicit merchandise in his garden, much to the disgust of the police who never found anything. One dark night he went out to get a bottle and, after pacing off the distance, began to dig. As he did so he was startled by a light so bright he had difficulty looking at it. The light approached, dimming as it came, and to his astonishment and terror he saw it was emitted by the huge eyes of a creature two metres tall, covered with black, short, hair.

The bootlegger, of course, stopped digging, and as soon as he did, the creature began to move away from him. The eyes dimmed as it went, and eventually went out altogether as the being disappeared into the distance. The bootlegger quickly filled in his hole and rushed back into his home. One suspects that he may have partaken of his own merchandise that evening.

Next evening, he ventured up to the garden once more. Locating the spot again, he nervously began to dig and instantly the light reappeared and approached him. He saw with relief that when he stopped digging the frightful creature moved away and its eyes dimmed.

The bootlegger again ceased his digging and returned to his house, and as often happens in folklore tales, the story has a moral ending. The man decided to give up his life of crime and seek other, less exciting forms of commerce.

The creature that approached this poor man certainly sounds like a Sasquatch—two metres tall and covered in short dark hair—but how do we explain those eyes. This was clearly not a case of eye shine. This fellow was trying not to be discovered, so he would hardly have been walking around in his garden with a lantern.

Also, the light is described as so bright that the bootlegger had trouble looking at it. Again, eye shine is not that bright, and, typically, beings with self-illuminating eyes fall firmly into the realm of the paranormal and even apparitional. For example, the Phantom Black Dogs, which I studied for another book, are frequently seen to have glowing eyes of varying colours, often red.

Taft notes that the story is uncorroborated, so we should not put too much stock in it. Nevertheless, there are other stories of Hairy Ones with glowing eyes, see Renner and Cutchin, so we cannot ignore the story simply because it does not fit our paradigm.

ANOTHER STRANGE STORY from *Where the Footprints End* comes out of Short Hills, Ontario. The account, from Albert Rosales' extensive humanoid encounter database, is short, so I will quote it in its entirety.

Two 14-year-old boys were playing in a conservation area when a huge Bigfoot type creature approached and picked them up. The creature took them onboard a landed disc shaped object. Inside, several short humanoids dressed like doctors examined them apparently putting an implant into one of them. The Bigfoot type creature was seen to sit on a large chair inside the object. Several wires were placed on its head, which led to another device nearby.

While this is the only Sasquatch-UFO story that I found in my research of Canadian cases, we have but to look south of the border to see that people like Stan Gordon, in Pennsylvania, have documented a number of such stories, and I cover at least one such tale in my book *Mysteries in the Mist.*

I am not of the opinion that UFOs are necessarily alien spacecraft come from another planet or even another galaxy to investigate the warlike featherless bipeds that inhabit this planet. What I do note, in my other work, is that there seems to be an intelligence behind UFOs and other strangeness. That intelligence seems bent on getting humans to observe these phenomena and even seems to produce a variety of phenomena to maximize the confusion or outright fear of the observers.

The Sasquatch or, at least, Sasquatch-like creatures seem to be one of the phenomena that appear in these little clusters as we see above. I found it interesting that the Hairy One in this story, once it had collected the two boys, seemed to lounge around, waiting for the "doctors" to be done. The detail of the wires placed on its head and running to another instrument was interesting even if we have no idea what this whole scenario means. This exceedingly bizarre story leads us into an outbreak of the strange that happened in Ontario and featured several Sasquatch-like creatures.

━━━

In *WHERE THE FOOTPRINTS END*, Timothy Renner and Joshua Cutchin tell a story that combines owls, UFOS, and Sasquatch that came to them from Mike Clelland's mind-blowing book *The Messengers: Owls, Synchronicity, and the UFO Abductee.* The subject of the story, Susan MacLeod, lived in Ontario and was of partial Mi'kmaq ancestry. This connection to an indigenous group is necessary background for understanding the story.

MacLeod stated in *The Messengers* that the summer of 2015 had seen her surrounded by owls. Clelland, in this work, establishes that anomalous owl sightings (large numbers of owls and/or "giant" owls or owls seen in places where they should not be) seem to have a much deeper meaning and to be related to the UFO abduction phenomenon.

The witness had undergone a painful dental procedure on August 15 and had gone out to a small tipi on her property for some quiet evening reflection and to mourn the passing of a friend. While she was there, she smelled a "damp musky odour" and heard something brushing against the side of the structure.

Disturbed by this event, MacLeod exited the tipi only to be confronted by "two red lights" and "multiple eyes reflecting back at her". She discerned five Sasquatch, two taller and three shorter, at a range of twenty feet. The woman retreated into the tipi but eventually made her way back to the house, noting that the group of Hairy Ones were still present but had moved to a more comfortable distance.

When MacLeod entered her home, however, her children were full of stories of shadow shapes "flying all through the house". When she checked in with her partner later in the evening, he had camped out in the garage, stating that he, too, had seen the mysterious shadow people.

MacLeod did not feel, given her family's fright over the seemingly paranormal experiences, that she could relate her Sasquatch experience, so she went out onto her driveway and began to pray, asking for divine assistance in dealing with this outbreak of oddity.

MacLeod had been looking up at what she thought were three stars, but the stars began to move and formed into a classic triangle-shaped UFO. Clelland reported:

> She called out to her partner, and he came running out to the opening along the driveway. He looked up to see these three colored lights slowly moving apart, but the stars within the triangle were being blotted out by something giant right above them. They both watched as something enormous began forming itself into a semi-solid kind of matter. It was right then that she understood that all these events, the Sasquatch, the shadow beings, and now this giant craft were somehow connected.

It is one thing to see a Sasquatch or have an experience of shadow people or to view a UFO, but to have all those things happen over one night again strains the limits of credulity. The question is: if Sasquatch is simply a flesh and blood animal, why does it sometimes appear in tandem with these other strange experiences?

BEFORE WE GET to more UFO strangeness, however, we must deal with another noted area of weirdness surrounding the

4

Sasquatch—the idea that the creature can transmit thoughts and feelings to human beings.

In Alberta Sasquatch report #041, we have a childhood observation of a Sasquatch that has a decidedly weird element to its otherwise ordinary narrative. In August of 1972, the witness and his family visited Strathcona Island Park in Medicine Hat, Alberta, so that they could have a family picnic. After getting a fire going, the family adjourned to the nearby river to swim.

At about 1330 hours, the family decided to move back to the campsite, about 150 yards away. The witness took off at speed, eager to get his first hot dog, and so ran ahead of the group.

The witness' first intimation of something unusual was, as is sometimes seen in these cases, a strong odour. He likened the smell to a newly washed dog that had been rolling in garbage for a week. The witness heard a movement in the brush to his right and spied a "large, black and red furred back" at a range of about thirty feet. Whatever he was looking at appeared to be squatting, as its buttocks were inches from the ground.

The being was hunched down over a Saskatoon berry bush, but it must have been quite large since, even squatting down, the witness states that it was four feet wide and five feet high. The creature had a "cone shaped head that seemed to be sitting on its shoulders".

So far, this incident sounds like any of a dozen Sasquatch sightings that we have seen in this book. The story takes a turn for the strange when the witness thought to himself, "What am I looking at?"

Something replied to him, in his mind. "You don't see me. I'm not here."

Again, the witness wondered what he was looking at, and, again, the creature spoke the same words into his mind.

The being then began to make a sort of chattering noise, and the witness described his mind being filled with the thought that he needed to leave, to get out of that area. The witness took off running to his campsite while the Sasquatch seems to have made for a nearby creek.

The witness' family pulled out the standard explanation for his sighting. He was told that he must have seen a bear. When he insisted that it was unlike any bear he had ever seen, the family jokingly told him that he had seen a Sasquatch. He didn't know what that was, and when someone explained the idea to him, he concluded that this was what he had seen.

Now, if the witness had just been overwhelmed with the desire to leave the area, a Sasquatch researcher might pull out the explanation of infrasound, the idea that certain animals can produce sounds that produce an emotional reaction in animals and humans. In this case, however, we can rule out infrasound since the witness actually heard the creature speaking in his mind.

It is possible that the last command, to leave the area, was boosted with infrasound, but that still leaves the psychic impression that told the witness he was not seeing what he was seeing. This story moves close to the idea of psychic manipulation. Is it possible that, after trying to manipulate the boy into not seeing it at all, the creature was then forced to run the youth off when he proved resistant to its manipulation?

If this happened to be true, then we would really have to alter our view of what Sasquatch is and what it is capable of.

IN ANOTHER PECULIAR CASE, this one out of Manitoba, Wes Germer of *Sasquatch Chronicles* interviewed a witness named Remee on episode 298.

Remee was a child at the time of the sighting, driving with his parents up to visit relatives in Northern Manitoba. At the time of the sighting, his father was driving their van, and his mother was asleep in the back.

The incident started as a near-typical roadside Sasquatch encounter, with the animal moving from a ditch and crossing the road in front of the van in a couple of strides. Remee described the animal as more massive than a bear, with long arms "like a gorilla". The hair on the arms was longer than the short hair on the body. The Sasquatch was more ape-like but with a more human-style physique, according to the witness. The animal was close enough for Remee to make out the "robust" facial features and the large, dark eyes.

It was the eyes that seem to have been Remee's undoing. Upon making eye contact with the creature, the witness stated:

> So in the instance when the Sasquatch stopped and stared at me I felt a great sadness, but like a loss or separation from another and a kind of lonely franticness almost like a driven search out of a panic. I also felt the Sasquatch's mentality was what we would equate to that of a late teen early adult years and that it was a highly intelligent male. I remember his eyes the most they were large and dark but had a soft sad/driven/frantic panic kind of feel. I really didn't feel he was any kind of threat or that he would want to be.

Remee owned the fact that he has empathic experiences in which he gets gut feelings about people and animals. A skeptic will, of course, dismiss this incident as the overactive imagination of a child, but I am not so quick to dismiss testimony from the young. More than one person interested in the esoteric has noted that children are more sensitive to psychic impressions than adults since they have not fully absorbed the Western scientific materialist paradigm that says that such things are impossible. In other words, they have not had psychism trained out of them yet.

Psychic abilities exist, despite the efforts of scientific materialists to ignore the mountain of evidence for their existence. If we take Remee at his word, then this experience is quite interesting. Not only does the witness indicate that Sasquatch are highly intelligent, but he also felt, unequivocally, that this individual was in distress. One might even extrapolate that it took the dangerous measure of crossing the road since it seemed to be looking for others of its kind. Why else would a Sasquatch be experiencing the sense of separation and panic that Remee felt from this animal?

Both the witness and his father saw the creature, and Remee was certain that it was not a bear. Interestingly, after the encounter, Remee's father refused to discuss the event at all. By the time of the interview, the father had developed dementia, so any hopes of getting him to corroborate his son's story had faded.

Now that we have seen Sasquatch establish communication with people's minds, let's look at a story about communication of a different sort.

———

JOHN WARMS, in his wonderful book *Strange Creatures Seldom Seen,* details another story of communication with a Sasquatch. Warms' book focuses on witnesses to cryptid encounters in Manitoba. Many of the percipients that he interviewed were First Nations folks.

Warms tells us the story of Mrs. Smith, whose family was camping on Landry Lake, a body of water set near the road that leads from The Pas to Moose Lake. The family had camped "beside the lake in a parking lot of a boat launch". Mrs. Smith woke to find that her young son was not in bed and so rose to look for him. She found the boy fishing along the shore and talked him into coming back to bed. They both smelled a distinct, "awful" odour in area and, assuming that it was a bear, retreated to the safety of camp. The two spoke openly about the awful smell before returning to their beds.

A few hours later, the witness awakened and went outside to smoke. She heard a splashing at the edge of the lake and walked, on bare feet, across the clearing to see what was making the sound. What she saw was:

> ... a big brown Sasquatch standing more than knee deep in the lake, pouring water over itself with its hands, alternating one after the other. It noticed her almost immediately, and cleared the distance to the bush in four or five big steps. It was almost as if it had heard mother and son discussing the terrible smell, and decided to take a bath—or rather, a shower. The experience did not prevent them from returning to the area, although a garter snake scared Mrs. Smith away from it on a subsequent visit.

While this story is amusing—a Sasquatch didn't scare the woman away from the area, but a garter snake did—it does give one pause. The presence of a distinct and often rotten odour is a staple of Sasquatch sightings. The creature is even called a skunk ape in Florida for this very reason, but this is the first time I have ever seen indication of a Sasquatch taking a bath after someone commented on its odiferous nature.

Now, I realize that the two events might simply be coincidental. The mother and son may have smelled something in the night, commented on it, and then the mother saw a Sasquatch seemingly bathing in the lake later on. Still, this seems to stretch the bounds of credulity. The odds against seeing a Sasquatch are already fairly high, even if one lives in the wilderness of Manitoba. The odds of seeing a Sasquatch performing an action that seemed to be in direct response to something you said earlier are almost astronomical.

If we take the road less travelled and assume that the creature could understand the people speaking about it, we are then left with a being that has language and, perhaps, can learn other languages. We've seen gorillas and other apes learning sign language and communicating effectively with humans. Might this be another extraordinary ability we can credit to the Sasquatch?

———

I SPOKE about the Snelgrove Lake sightings and the *MonsterQuest* episodes that documented them in the Ontario section of the book. While I was reading about the incident and then watching the video, I came across an oddity that no one seems to have noticed in all the excitement over the possible DNA evidence from the screw board.

Doug Hajicek, the producer of the *MonsterQuest* series, appeared on *Sasquatch Chronicles* (episode 312) and related a peculiar incident that occurred while he was in residence at the cabin some time before the events of the *MonsterQuest* episodes.

Hajicek and his companions had experienced a wood knock earlier in the day. The group waited until late at night and then did a knock of their own, which was answered immediately. One of the group threw a rock in the direction of the knock, and the rock was returned, gently. Rocks kept coming for an hour or so, but no vocalization or further wood knocks were heard.

Eventually, members of the party tired and decided to go to

bed. Hajicek chose to stay up for a while, reading, until he, too, began to grow sleepy. He turned on the light in the kitchen, presumably to make his nightly ablutions, and "all hell broke loose".

Abruptly, there was the sound of running on the roof, stones began to fall again, and the cabin began to shake violently, as though something were trying to take it off its foundation. Hajicek conjectured that he had startled the local Sasquatch when he turned on the light, but, regardless, the peculiar thing is that, during all this commotion, not one of his companions awoke despite the producer's best efforts to rouse them.

I talked extensively about what UFO researcher Jenny Randles called the Oz Factor in my book *Mysteries in the Mist*. Randles theorized that there were certain effects that could be seen preceding or in conjunction with a UFO sighting, and paranormal researchers have gone on to note that these effects are often seen around other phenomenon, including some Sasquatch sightings.

The classic Oz Factor signs are a sense that something is about to happen, the fading out of ambient noise and a feeling that time is not proceeding at its normal pace, or at all. In general, it seems that the witness is somewhat out of sync with the rest of the world, and this effect seems to occur in a zone around the witness. Randles first noted it in a UFO case where one security guard had a full-blown UFO experience while another, nearby, as well as people in houses all around the sighting area, did not.

This seems to be what happened with Hajicek. While he was experiencing the terror of the seeming attack, his cabin mates were able to slumber soundly, and, in fact, he could not wake them up. This is very reminiscent of the experience of UFO abductees who have frightening events unfold around them in the night while their bed partner remains firmly asleep.

Researchers tend to silo. That is, they develop an interest in one area of study and specialize in that, often being unaware or even ignoring other areas of study. This is especially true of Sasquatch researchers who, convinced that they are hunting a flesh and blood creature, often are unaware of work in the paranormal and ufology. I suspect that many Sasquatch researchers consider these fields to be too "woo" for their taste, and this leads to stories like the one above slipping through the cracks.

Hajicek wondered if his cabin mates were simply exhausted from the day and slept through the event. Somehow, I think that there might have been far more going on, but let's continue with our parade of Sasquatch strangeness.

IN LINE with the very Oz Factor occurrence in the previous story, we also have BFRO report #16779, which occurs in the summer of 1992. The witness, a self-proclaimed "sort of explorer kind of person", had decided to take a walk on a dirt road leading west from his home near Whitehorse into dense and sometimes rocky forest. He walked for over an hour, hoping to come across an abandoned cabin or even a change of scenery, to no avail.

The witness, whom we later discover is named Bill, pointed out that, while he did not have any frightened or odd feelings, he noticed the extreme silence of the forest as he moved along that day. Those familiar with the woodland know that it is seldom completely quiet, even at night when many creatures are abed.

The subject got home as night fell, and nothing further occurred that day.

In the morning, Bill told his mother about an old dump site he had seen along the way and asked if she would like to come check it out. The mother was, apparently, a collector of old bottles, and her son thought she might find something of interest in the dump.

The mother agreed, and the two made their way to the dump site. The mother had no luck finding bottles for her collection but had enjoyed the walk and even managed to gather some flowers. The son proposed that they walk a little farther on the road, and, oddly, the mother commented that she was alright with this as long as there were no bears around. The witness told her that he hadn't seen any and went on to comment that he had never had trouble with bears in that area before.

The two then proceeded down the road but only got a short distance before the young man stopped in his tracks. His mother stopped too, about fifty feet behind him. The following is edited slightly for spelling and punctuation:

> I turn to her and say someone is up ahead. I look again and there he is. I expect him to approach and say hi or whatever. It doesn't happen. I look closer. The sun is behind him, and he is in the shade of the trees. (The sun is never high up here.) I notice that this guy, besides being unusually big and tall, is also wearing black coveralls, and he has a huge mop of hair tapering from the top of his head to the outside of his shoulders. Now I'm standing in the middle of the road my bright purple T-shirt is glowing almost neon bright in the sunshine. I'm waiting for him to approach, and I'm staring at him, trying to see the face, the eyes. Nothing. He's still swaying from side to side a bit but otherwise just standing there. My mom is still about 50 feet back, and she is staying there. She doesn't want to approach any further. She is saying, "What, what is it, Bill?" I say, "I'm not sure."

After about three minutes of staring at this figure and it

seeming to stare back at him, Bill was beginning to realize that he was not looking at a human. Subsequent to that notion was the thought that he did not want his mother seeing the object of his attention. As he put it, he wanted "no screaming, no jumping, no fainting and no running".

The witness considered approaching the figure but felt that he should not, only to have the figure begin to approach him. At this point, the witness decided to retreat, and taking his mother in hand, he began to walk quickly back the way they had come.

Bill looked back at each corner the duo passed and sighted the creature at the third corner. At a range of about twenty feet, he described the creature as "huge" with a pronounced crest that reminded the witness of the Coneheads of *Saturday Night Live*. Again, he noted that it was "extremely quiet" and that he does not recall hearing the normal forest sounds one would expect to hear on a summer's day.

To add to the strangeness of this sighting, Bill stated that when the creature walked, it was liked it "levitated. Like he wasn't touching the ground but a few inches above it". If that wasn't odd enough, the witness also stated that the creature "seemed to have no definition. Just like a shadow".

Bill stated that the creature took two steps and then was "gone in the woods". He hurried his mother along until they reached the main road, and then the two stopped, sat on a log, and shared a sandwich. Bill told his mother what he had seen, and she asked if he was sure, which he was.

The witness also noted, in his report, that he could not understand why the Yukon was not considered a "hot spot" for what he called "bushmen". Apparently, the Natives in that region were very aware of the Sasquatch, and the creature came into their village on a regular basis.

As I noted in the previous section, one of the three signs of what Jenny Randles called the Oz Factor is the fading away of ambient noise. We see this sign of a paranormal incursion twice in this story, once when Bill is out walking by himself the day before the sighting, and once when Bill and his mother encounter the Sasquatch.

What I call the Silence, coupled with the indistinct nature of this Sasquatch, more shadow-like than solid and physical, really gives me pause in examining this account. It should be noted that, unlike some stories, where the creatures disappear into the bush with accompanying branch snaps and movement sounds, this Sasquatch made absolutely no noise during the entire encounter.

IN AN INTERESTING DOCUMENTARY entitled *Sasquatch on Lake Superior*, narrator Dee McCullay tells the brief story of two hunters who were staked out in a spot not far from Ontario Highway 11 near a place called Deadman's Curve. Upon hearing the snapping of branches in the bush, the two were surprised to see a classic Sasquatch, covered in long dark hair but wearing coveralls like those one would see on a mechanic.

This sighting is so odd that I will simply leave it and not comment, except to say that coveralls have not been noted as a Sasquatch fashion accessory in most books I have read.

IN "AN INTERVIEW WITH A SASQUATCH RESEARCHER", the *Alberta Sasquatch* website has an interesting account of one of these creatures, again seen near Whitehorse in the Yukon. The researcher in question is asked what their most interesting report was, and the reply is worth quoting.

In the summer of 2010, here in Whitehorse, a gentleman friend of mine was driving downtown on Azure Road to do some shopping when he noticed something walking on the right-hand side ditch. He slowed down and observed a Sasquatch two metres (seven-to-eight feet) tall walking in a southern direction at a slow, dedicated pace. He slowed down his car and followed the Sasquatch for a distance of some 30 metres.

The Sasquatch did not even look at him and seemed not to notice the car only two meters beside him and paid no attention to it. The Sasquatch acted like a man on a mission, not paying attention to anything else at all. Some five metres before a utility pole the Sasquatch started losing its overall shape, becoming gradually transparent to the point, as the witness stated to me on many occasions, that the witness could see right through it, yet its overall form was still outlining his transparent body, as the Sasquatch reached the utility pole, he totally disappeared from sight.

I have investigated this sighting on many occasions and talked to the witness about it many times. I walked and measured the sighting location and even looked for a "portal" or something like it and I am still baffled.

Once again, as noted in the section on Sasquatch road sightings, we have a Hairy One completely ignoring a motor vehicle at close range and going about its business in a steady and determined manner. Then it literally fades from view, becoming transparent before disappearing completely. Such a trick is not within the purview of a flesh and blood creature, and such vanishing acts are not unique.

While I have tried to keep the reports for this book within Canadian borders, I feel it is incumbent on me to note that Sasquatch vanishing in front of a witness have been noted in other cases. For example, in the classic text *Alien Animals*, Janet and Colin Bord relate the story of a witness who lived near Uniontown, Pennsylvania. The woman heard a noise on her front porch and, thinking that feral dogs were about, took a loaded shotgun to investigate.

The witness turned on her porch light, opened the door and stepped out only to be confronted by a seven-foot-tall "hairy ape", which raised its arms upon seeing her. The woman, certain she was about to be attacked, fired her weapon into the creature's middle. The being "just disappeared in a flash of light".

To add to the strangeness of that Pennsylvania encounter, the woman's son, who heard the gunshot and came to assist, saw several other creatures in the woods. All were described as seven feet tall and hairy, with long arms that came down to their knees. The creatures were also said to have eyes that glowed red, even in total darkness.

Needless to say, primates do not vanish into thin air, and there is no known example of a primate with self-illuminating eyes. To drive home this issue of disappearing Sasquatch, let's look at a story from the Yukon in which a pair of Sasquatch seem to understand sign language before making themselves scarce.

━━

IN A REPORT TO *SASQUATCHCANADA*, investigator Red Grossinger gives the account of a Yukon witness who encountered two of the creatures on Duncan Creek. The witness was a gentleman who was en route to a mining concern in Keno City to conduct hearing tests for the miners.

The man was ahead of schedule, and rather than proceeding to the mine where he was expected the next day, he decided to stop and camp overnight in the area of Duncan

Creek. He stopped for the night about 1600 hours and, after completing paperwork, prepared dinner and then decided to go for a leisurely hike along the stream.

The witness hiked out, and then, as he rounded a turn on his way back to his campsite, he encountered two bipedal creatures at a range of ten metres (thirty-three feet). The animals were walking toward him, and both he and the beings stopped as they spotted each other.

The witness immediately noticed that one of the Sasquatch, for he had no doubt that is what they were, was heavily pregnant. This female stepped behind what the witness presumed was the male. That individual was grimacing in an "unpleasant manner" but had not made a sound.

The witness, of course, was shocked but decided that he had best try to communicate with the pair. He made a hand gesture, as though shaking hands and then touching his heart, three times. The witness said that he was trying to convey that he was not a threat.

The male Sasquatch seemed to understand and took on a less threatening demeanour. The witness then gestured at the clouds, trying to indicate that rain was coming, then toward the brush, off the path. He hoped to relate that he would give way to the Sasquatch and walk off the trail, but when he tried to do this, the two creatures "stepped off the trail to their left and in the blink of an eye they were no longer visible".

Let's be quite clear here. The witness is not saying that the animals blended into the forest. He is saying that they vanished from sight, and they could not be heard moving through the woods.

The gentleman stated that he could not see them any longer. The forest was not that thick and that two large creatures like them would have been visible for a while anyway. But such was not the case. He then further mentioned that he had not heard any walking sounds whatsoever, even though anything walking in the bush would have made some sounds, but in this case it was total silence.

In this section we have seen a ghost that looked like a gorilla, a seeming Sasquatch with flaming eyes, a Hairy One that appeared from a UFO and examples of Sasquatch communicating mind to mind and seeming to understand human speech. Now we have Sasquatch that appear to understand sign language and then vanish without a trace.

I think it is fair to say that we have established that something strange is happening in some portion of Sasquatch sightings. As we ponder what this means, let's take a look at what some of the indigenous people of North America believe about these creatures.

CHAPTER EIGHT
NATIVE BELIEFS

AS I NOTED in the introduction, First Nations people are often reluctant to speak about the creature we call Sasquatch. John Warms, in his book *Strange Creatures Seldom Seen,* speaks about the elders of an area telling people not to discuss their sightings. They had seen something that was a mystery and should leave well enough alone, keeping the wonder of that mystery to themselves. There is something to be said for this attitude, from a spiritual perspective, but it does not help those of us trying to understand what Sasquatch is and what the First Nations people know or believe about the Hairy One.

Yet, at times, even the elders will speak, if only to verify that the creature does, indeed, exist. In an article on the *Alberta Sasquatch* blog, the author, a maker of documentaries, spoke with an elder of the Tsuu T'ina people, a Dené tribe in southern Alberta that became part of the Blackfoot Confederacy.

This woman told a story about her husband and a friend who had gone hunting in the foothills of the Rockies. The hunt had been successful, and the two were in the process of skinning and dressing an animal when the husband noticed "something watching them from a distance". Moving slowly, the hunter looked up and realized that he was looking at a Sasquatch, "hairy, with a man-like appearance" which was, in turn, staring back at him.

The husband seemed to know exactly how to react. Speaking quietly to his friend, he let his fellow hunter know about the creature "they all knew and heard about". The husband surmised that his observer might be hungry, so he cut off a large piece of meat and handed it to the friend. The other hunter was instructed to keep his eyes down while the husband guided him to a tree where the Hairy One was waiting. The hunters would leave the meat on the branches of the tree.

Following instructions to the letter, the other hunter placed the meat and came back to resume dressing the prey animal. "They carried on as if everything was normal." When they were prepared to take the meat out, they looked up to find the Sasquatch and the meat gone!

Interestingly, the elder, when she had finished telling this story, looked up at the filmmaker and said, "UFOs, Sasquatch and Little People, these three are real." The author of the piece notes that having an elder tell her this made her more open to "the unknown and the mysterious", and I think this might be a lesson we need to take away from this account and the beliefs of Native folk.

One cannot speak of First Nations people as a block. There are many different indigenous groups with a wide variety of beliefs. In general, though, those who follow traditional tribal beliefs do not suffer from the quandary that many people in the West face. They have not been raised on a steady diet of scientific materialism that tells them there is nothing more than what they can perceive with their five senses (or instrumentation designed for those five senses).

In the excellent documentary film *Sasquatch'n*, we encounter First Nations people from a number of different tribes and areas speaking of the creature we are calling Sasquatch. I found it interesting that there were a couple of well-known, non-Native researchers in the film, and both sounded the same note.

Dr. John Bindernagel, for example, noted in his segment of the film that Sasquatch is a part of Native culture, a part that "white people" tend to dismiss as made up. Bindernagel did not accept the notion that First Nations people were simply making up this creature but instead suggested that the indigenous people were describing the exact same thing that "white people" were seeing. The doctor then went on to display track casts and other seemingly physical evidence of the Hairy One. Binder-nagel expressed the idea that we of the West are arrogant, noting that there is a wide gulf between us and animals, whereas Native people often rely, at least in part, on their knowledge of the creatures around them for their very survival.

The other noted Sasquatch researcher who appears in the film, Kathy Moskowitz-Strain, is well known for her work *Giants, Cannibals and Monsters*, in which she details various First Nations myths of the Sasquatch throughout North America. This researcher noted that Native people are taught to view the Hairy One (or whatever his local name happened to be) with respect. Often, the Sasquatch is viewed as a guardian of the forest or wildlands, according to Moskowitz-Strain.

Listening to the testimony of various First Nations people in the film, we quickly become aware that these people do not view the Sasquatch as a simple animal. Vera Newman, a Namgis elder, tells us that Tsonoqua, their word for the crea-ture, is the "Wild Woman of the Woods", and those from the Namgis tribe who have seen her always refer to the Sasquatch as female. The narrator of the film tells us that Tsonoqua has a smaller, male companion called the Bukwas.

These beings, in the area of British Columbia where most of

the documentary was filmed, are an integral part of the Native culture. The Sasquatch appears on totem poles and throughout the myths of the indigenous people, and their attitude toward the creature is very simple—an encounter with Sasquatch is a sacred event.

According to Jonathan Brewer, another First Nations person appearing in the film, seeing a Sasquatch is an "epic blessing", and the commercialism that has surrounded the creature in "white" culture is a slap in the face to Native people. "You are not honouring us in any way ..." Brewer says at one point in the film.

Joey Poorthunder, a Diné person, comes to the heart of the matter when he tells the film crew that the Sasquatch is a "Higher Power and high spirits of the mountains, grandmothers and grandfathers, who we [the tribe] come from ... our lineage comes from ... long ago, we were all one nation. If we saw one, we would make prayers, make offerings". We see Poorthunder's words echoed in the actions of the hunters described above. It is common, in animistic cultures, to make offerings to the spirits of the land.

Kelsey Charlie tells us that the songs about the Sasquatch are so old that their origins have been lost to history. "We know that they are a part of it and it is a part of us ... it's something sacred", a supernatural being that has been with his tribe for thousands of years. Charlie had a sighting of his own, and when he recognized what he was looking at, he simply thanked the creature for allowing him to see it and its young.

Charlie goes on to say that the people most likely to see one of these beings are people who are in the right place, at the right time with the right [presumably reverent] attitude. He states definitively that no one will ever capture a Sasquatch since the creature lives in "two realms" and can move easily from one realm to the other. In addition, Charlie maintains that the creature can shape-shift.

I'll speak more about this more spiritual interpretation of Sasquatch later in the book.

Such sentiments about the sacredness of Sasquatch are not just found in the afore-mentioned documentary. In an article for *Sudbury.com*, Bill Steer spoke extensively with Indigenous knowledge keeper and cultural teacher Dr. Jonathan Pitt. The doctor is of Anishinabek and Haudenosaunee heritage and tells us:

> In our traditional teachings of the Seven Grandfathers:
> Gwekwaadziwin (Honesty) is often connected with Sabe
> [author's note: Sasquatch in Dr. Pitt's language], as all of the
> teachings are, however, the other six are connected with such
> other animals such as Mukwa (bear) or Migizi (eagle), in my
> mind having Honesty not connected with a something not
> present in the world does not make sense.

Dr. Pitt also notes that his understanding is that Sabe "could be an inter-dimensional being and able to move within spaces". This elder then goes on to say:

> One Indigenous Elder once said that there are areas where the
> Sabe live and we do not go there, we live here and they live there
> and he used to walk among us. It is a common understanding
> amongst Native peoples that if we don't bother Sabe in his habitat
> he won't bother us in suburbia; best left that way in my mind if
> researchers think they could grow to over seven and a half feet.

In Dr. Pitt's view, the oral history of some Native communities views Sasquatch as a guardian and protector of Mother

Earth, a peaceful creature when left alone. The Hairy One is also often connected with water and seen as a water protector.

The good doctor finishes his statement by saying:

> I am of the bear clan and I view Mukwa as a protector and strength. I think if I did see a Sasquatch, I would avoid making eye contact (this advice I have been given by my Elders). It's my sense that Sabe perhaps chooses to be anti-social and stay away from humans because of how we treat each other and Mother Earth. Maybe one day if we are ready, Sabe may come out of hiding?

Maybe, indeed.

While it is true that many First Nations people view the creature we call Sasquatch as a sort of wilderness or water guardian, a reading of Kathy Moskowitz-Strain's *Giants, Cannibals and Monsters* reveals that some Native people did not have such a prosaic view of the forest giants. Some of the myths that Moskowitz-Strain brings forward seem to indicate a darker side to these creatures. According to those legends, the creatures were often guilty of kidnapping members of the tribe, and some of the scarier myths indicated that these beings were not above using humans as a food source.

Given what we have seen above about the Sasquatch being considered sacred by many tribes, one wonders why certain tribes developed a more adversarial relationship with these beings. I don't want to conjecture about why the Sasquatch in some areas seemed hostile to the local Natives, so I will close this section with an interesting note from the *Sasquatch'n* documentary referenced above.

Several times throughout the film, Native people stated flatly that the Sasquatch is trying to warn us about our lack of respect for Mother Earth. The Diné, as noted earlier, see the creature as a guardian of forest and mountains and a leader of the people in those spots. By people, the Native folk do not mean just humans. In their animistic worldview, people refers to the animals, plants and other spirits that inhabit an area. There are bear people, for instance, and oak people and stone people and so on.

Increased sightings of this creature, according to Native belief, may be tied to the fact that we are rapidly making this planet uninhabitable through our ceaseless and mindless consumption. Native people point out that we two-legged folk need to move back toward a way of connection, a way of inter-dependence, and that the Sasquatch is pointing the way for us.

Whether we believe the words and warnings of Native people in this regard, it is certainly true that the Sasquatch, to them, is a mysterious and sacred creature. It is these thoughts from Native people that give me pause and cause me to think there is more to Sasquatch than a simple relict hominid or new ape species.

It is also these thoughts that set me firmly in the "no kill" camp. My intuitive feeling of these creatures lines up with that of the Diné, who believe that the Hairy One may be even smarter than people. Many Native people believe that the Sasquatch viewed the encroaching colonization of the continent as a lack of respect for the earth, and thus they moved deeper into the wilderness. If it is true that a Sasquatch has human-level intellect or better, then, to me, shooting one would be the killing of a sentient being. I cannot support such a taking of life, even if science demands it.

Enough grim conjecture, however, let's move on to another interesting and possibly paranormal aspect of the Sasquatch phenomenon.

CHAPTER NINE
FOREST POLTERGEIST

THOSE READING to this point may have noted that all the sightings I have documented thus far are visual sightings. There exist, of course, what the Bigfoot Field Researchers Organization (BFRO) calls Class B sightings, that is, those encounters with something in the wilderness that do not yield a visual sighting. A Class B sighting may also be indicative of the presence of certain signs that some researchers feel indicate the presence of Sasquatch in the area.

The sources for these signs of Sasquatch in the area are so numerous that I cannot list them all here, but a look at a book like Ken Gerhard's *The Essential Guide to Bigfoot* should begin to put the reader on the right track. My own compilation of such indicators is as follows:

1) **The Silence**: witnesses and investigators often note that the surrounding woodland becomes eerily quiet in the presence of Sasquatch. We've talked about this in the previous section on strange things related to the forest giants and the so-called Oz Factor.

2) **Sounds of movement in the brush**: witnesses often

believe that a deer, elk, or moose is about to emerge. Sometimes, this phenomenon then yields a visual sighting while at other times nothing is seen.

3) **Heavy, supposedly bipedal footsteps**: it is a common statement amongst experiencers that they can tell the difference between the sound of a quadruped and a biped walking. Again, though footsteps may be a precursor to a visual sighting, these sounds are often the only evidence that something was there.

4) **Behaviour beyond the ken of an ordinary animal**: a good example of this was an experience in which some campers returned to their campsite to find their pots, which had been carefully nested together when the group left, set out individually. This group assumed that the culprit was a Sasquatch since they had come back to camp as the result of vocalizations heard while they were out.

5) **Rock throwing**: this one is self-explanatory and, as many witnesses say, puzzling since bears and other animals do not throw rocks.

6) **Wood knocking**: wood knocking has been recognized as a behaviour amongst great apes, and Sasquatch researchers point to this commonly observed sign as indicative of something (besides humans) with hands in the forest.

7) **Structures**: in some reports, lodge pole pines and trees are found bent, uprooted, or stacked in patterns such as woven or crisscross configurations. Researchers have theorized that these structures may represent shelters, in some cases, or territorial markers.

8) **Suspension of items in trees**: in one article for a publication called *Mountain Outlaw*, the writer tells of people finding deer carcasses suspended at height in the local woodland. None of the predators indigenous to North America are known to engage in the stowing of carcasses in trees.

9) **Creation of "nests" on the ground**: some researchers feel that massive depressions and arrangements of grasses and other detritus on the ground constitute proof of nesting Sasquatch in the area, perhaps thinking of similar structures used by mountain gorillas and other great apes.

10) **Vocalizations**: over the years, experiencers and researchers have recorded a variety of seemingly vocal sounds ranging from grunts, growls, and "chatter" to full-fledged howls.

11) **Footprints**: something with very large feet is leaving massive tracks in wild places and in conditions that make hoaxing very unlikely.

Now the problem with all of these "proofs" of the existence of Sasquatch is that they have not and will not be accepted by the scientific materialist establishment as evidence of the existence of a new great ape species or relict hominid. While I find this mass of circumstantial evidence proof that there is something out in the forest, I cannot take it as evidence that the something is necessarily Sasquatch.

Think of all the "Bigfoot" documentaries you have seen. In some of those films, such as the *Monsterquest* "Sasquatch Attacks" episode, there is clearly something in the woods throwing rocks at the film crew. Despite having both infrared and night-vision equipment, these film makers were unable to determine what the culprit was. We see the same thing occurring in the ever-popular *Finding Bigfoot*. The merry band of researchers have, on occasion, activity around their team, but, despite modern technology, they are never able to document a Sasquatch on film.

Somewhere in North America, as I am writing this, there are people out in the bush seeking to document the existence of Sasquatch or even, in extreme cases, to bring a body back for science. To date, those efforts have had very mixed results, and they certainly have not risen to the level of scientific proof.

It's one thing for a creature to evade the clutches of science when it is assumed extinct or there is no one looking for it but quite another thing for a being to evade the efforts of a dedicated group of humans who are constantly seeking it. I don't think anyone has an exact count of the number of groups and individuals who are actively seeking the Hairy One, but I should think these people would number into the thousands. Add to that the hunters who are constantly roaming the wilds of North America with weapons capable of bringing down a large animal and hikers with high-definition cameras in their phones and we should have something more than blurry images and circumstantial evidence to indicate the existence of Sasquatch.

The Sasquatch researcher will splutter at this, so I will reiterate my earlier point. I believe that (a) witnesses are seeing what they are seeing (more on that later) and (b) people in the wilderness are encountering something that is producing all the above signs of Sasquatch activity.

Podcaster Timothy Renner of the *Strange Familiars* podcast has noted on several occasions that, if you took all the signs that people are interpreting as the presence of Sasquatch and moved them into your house, you would have a classic poltergeist case. After looking at the lore of the poltergeist, I must agree.

Not being a poltergeist or haunting expert, I went to a basic book, Tom Ogden's *The Complete Idiot's Guide to Ghosts and Hauntings,* for some basic information. According to the Merriam-Webster dictionary online, the term poltergeist derives from the German and literally means "a knocking spirit" (from the verb *poltern*—to knock—and *geist*—a ghost or spirit). Ogden tells us that the poltergeist "tend[s] to be more destructive in their behaviour than ghosts. They're especially known for *throwing stones ...*" (emphasis mine).

As we scroll down the list of poltergeist accomplishments in Ogden's book, we quickly come across several items that should pique our interest. Poltergeists are known to cause various loud noises, including knocks and footsteps. As noted, these manifestations are well known for throwing rocks and for smashing or moving around items in the kitchen or even making items disappear and then reappear. Poltergeists are noisy things producing a range of vocalizations, including "whispers, cries, shrieks, moans, explosions, crashes and even recognizable and understandable speech".

Janet and Colin Bord, in their *Modern Mysteries of the World*, give us further food for thought. Experiencers have told stories of something heavily striking the side of their home or cabin. The Bords note that in a poltergeist outbreak in 1913 France, residents of a home in Fougères-sur-Bièvre reported that when they struck "a definite number of blows on the wall. Immediately a similar number would answer, but with a peculiar sonorousness". Sasquatch researchers often try to get their subject to reply to wood knocks, but the above case indicates that it may not be the Hairy One making the knocks.

The Bords also note that, while the poltergeist is certainly capable of flinging stone, this phenomenon also seems quite capable of simply apporting stones into a space and causing them to fall on or near people. Such incidents were reported in poltergeist outbreaks in Poona, India, Vachendorf, Germany, and Nickelheim, Germany.

Poltergeists also seem capable of moving quite large objects. In an outbreak in Pearisburg, Virginia, the police officer who investigated noted that the furniture that had moved around the house weighed two hundred pounds or more. In his report, the officer noted that the items were so heavy that the mother in the incident and her child could not have moved the items even if they had both been working together.

The Bords also note that the phenomenon seems to have a certain intelligence and will sometimes respond to requests to return an item, or in the case of William Roll, the parapsychologist, will make a liar of a person. Roll told people in a poltergeist case that these phenomena do not hit people and was promptly hit in the head by a small bottle, which had been standing on a nearby table.

Additionally, in the Poona, India, case, the Bords found an example of someone leaving out fruit for the "spirits" to eat. "The fruit disappeared and sounds of eating were heard, with lip-smacking noises. Then the rinds reappeared, bearing tooth-marks." Researchers have left gifts of food out for Sasquatch, and those items often go missing in the night, without triggering watching trail cams.

Keeping all this in mind, let's go back over our list and see how the poltergeist measures up.

---

1) **The Silence**: I have noted in *Mysteries in the Mist* that silence descending in an area is a sign that a paranormal incursion of some sort may be occurring. This phenomenon was first documented by Jenny Randles in what she called the Oz Factor around UFO sightings and has been noted by other researchers in the paranormal world.

2) **Sounds of movement in the brush**: a force that is capable of moving two-hundred-pound furniture is surely able to make some noise in the bush.

3) **Heavy, supposedly bipedal footsteps**: bipedal footsteps are a hallmark of poltergeist encounters and, indeed, have been noted in other types of hauntings.

4) **Behaviour beyond the ken of an ordinary animal**:

as I noted above, the poltergeist does seem to possess an intelligence. It is known to cause things to appear and disappear on request, open all the cabinet doors in a kitchen and then close them to scare the residents, and even respond in a yes and no fashion to knocks on wood (see wood knocks below).

5) **Rock throwing**: again, this is a hallmark sign of a poltergeist infestation.

6) **Wood knocking**: the history of the Spiritualist movement began with the Fox sisters in New York State, communicating with a spirit using knocking on a table. The sisters developed a code, and the intelligence with which they were communicating responded using that code. Knocks, bangs and rapping noises are, again, hallmarks of the poltergeist phenomenon.

7) **Structures**: if an intelligent force is inhabiting the forest and it is capable of moving things around to suit itself, then why not arrange trees in a manner that pleases it? Poltergeists seem to have some of the devil in them, and such actions could simply be mischief put forward to puzzle researchers.

8) **Suspension of items in trees**: see my comments under Structures. This behaviour, too, could be a touch of mischief on the part of the "forest poltergeist".

9) **Creation of "nests" on the ground**: I didn't encounter anything in the research on poltergeists that indicates that they would make nests, but, again, a force capable of moving furniture should be capable of arranging these nests.

10) **Vocalizations**: over the years, poltergeist experiencers have documented a number of different sounds that these spirits —if that is what they are—can make. I see no reason why a poltergeist, wild and free in the woodland, might not express itself in several interesting ways.

11) **Footprints**: Colin Wilson, in his study of poltergeists, noted that, in the Bell Witch case, the "witch"—a seemingly

malevolent poltergeist-type energy—actually made footprints appear in the snow for John Bell Junior after the death of his father. An old ghost-hunting trick involves spreading flour or some other dusty substance around a haunting to see if something leaves footprints. So, again, these prints could as easily be left by our mysterious poltergeist force as by a large hairy hominid or ape.

———

WHAT IS A POLTERGEIST? Parapsychologists are still going around in circles about the exact nature of the poltergeist phenomenon.

It used to be popular to theorize that the poltergeist was actually an outbreak of spontaneous psychokinetic activity. Parapsychologists noted, in many poltergeist cases, the presence of children, particularly pre-pubescent and pubescent youngsters. The hypothesis was that, for whatever reason, these children were suppressing their emotions around this turbulent time in their lives and that those emotions were expressing themselves in spontaneous outbreaks in which their minds were moving matter (psychokinesis).

Psychokinesis is one of the effects of the mind that has been proven in double-blind experiments but not at the level required for a poltergeist outbreak. While I don't dismiss the idea, and it certainly seems that it could be true in some or even most cases, I think that we have to remember that there are more things in heaven and earth than are met with in the philosophy of the scientific Horatios.

Animists, throughout history, have noted the presence of a massive and diverse ecosystem of spirits in what we will call the Otherworld. Some of those spirits were able to make their way onto our plane and, in some instances, wreak havoc. We have only to read books like Evans-Wentz' *The Fairy Faith in Celtic Countries* or one of Katharine Briggs' numerous treatises on the faery to understand that, when angered, these spirits were quite capable of producing the poltergeist effect.

Given the association in folklore of a wide range of spirits with the wilderness, it seems entirely possible that some spiritual agency is creating the effects that people associate with the presence of Sasquatch.

So why do I even bring this up? I've just spent a number of pages documenting sightings of a creature in the woods, and I've said that I believe that people are seeing something unusual. What I want to show here is that, while a certain percentage of people see a Sasquatch after experiencing some of this "forest poltergeist" phenomenon, many people do not and are unable, even with modern equipment, to track the source of their disturbance. This inability to track the source of the disturbance seems to lend itself to a more spiritual or psychic explanation, and I will discuss this in some depth in the conclusion.

It seems to me, and to some other researchers, that there is more to the Sasquatch than a simple flesh and blood creature wandering undiscovered in the forests of the world. My conclusions on the matter of Sasquatch are very much based in the visual sightings that I have documented above **and** in the other reports of far stranger happenings around the creatures. I also take into account the beliefs of First Nations people as well as the above information on poltergeists.

This is not a phenomenon that lends itself to easy answers, and in my conclusion, I will look at how both/and thinking will serve researchers as they move forward in their exploration of this fascinating creature.

AFTERWORD

WHAT IS SASQUATCH?

As always happens when I research a book, I have more questions than answers as I come to the end of the text. The one question that everyone seems to want to answer is: what is Sasquatch? The answer, though, is one that does not satisfy: we don't know.

Despite their best efforts, Sasquatch hunters have not been able to offer the body of one of these creatures on the dissecting altar of science and science. For the most part, the scientific establishment has completely ignored this subject.

Part of the reason for this turning away from the subject is simply ignorance. Scientists are unwilling to look at the mass of evidence that indicates that there is something unusual being seen out in the woodlands of North America and beyond. This unwillingness is sometimes a matter of predetermined thought patterns amongst science professionals (this thing cannot exist; therefore it does not exist) or, worse, scientists are looking at so-called fringe elements of the Sasquatch world that are making dubious claims about this animal (Sasquatch is an alien, for example) and deciding that it safest to ignore the whole issue.

As I mentioned in the introduction, I was hesitant to take up this subject, not because I worry about controversy, but because of the rancour with which proponents of various Sasquatch theories go at each other. It often seems that those who espouse certain theories are convinced that theirs is the One True Way, and those who do not believe as they do are blasphemers who deserve to be cast into the outer darkness.

The problem, as I see it, is one that I first brought up in *Phantom Black Dogs*. Researchers in the Sasquatch community are engaged in either/or thinking. Sasquatch must either be this thing, or one is completely mistaken, and it is some other thing. It occurs to me that what is needed in the discourse about the forest giants is a healthy dose of both/and thinking.

For example, I am completely in agreement that the witnesses to this phenomenon are seeing something in the woods and are having very real experiences. It also seems to be the case that the being that is being observed is quite capable of interacting with its physical environment, just as you or I might.

Where I differ from the flesh and blood hypothesis is in the thought that this is the only possible explanation for Sasquatch. Perusal of books like *Where the Footprints End* and even the section of strange things in this book make one note that a certain weirdness seems to envelop certain encounters with the Hairy One. Add to this the oddity of people having experiences of stone throwing, vocalizations and other manifestations that do not lead to a visual sighting and we have a phenomenon that closely resembles the poltergeist of paranormal lore.

So which is it? Is Sasquatch a physical but highly secretive being that exists in the forest, waiting for some lucky researcher to drop a net over it and bring it in for examination. Or is the Hairy One a supernatural or even alien creature capable of walking between the worlds, appearing and disappearing at will, speaking mind to mind and other extraordinary occurrences?

My answer to this is: yes.

Reading through the weight of sightings that I found in Canada, I was struck by how prosaic most of them are. If you substitute the word black bear for Sasquatch in a lot of these sightings, it seems that the witness encountered an animal in the woods, an animal just like the black bear or the moose or even the wolf. The only difference is that these other animals are known, and the Sasquatch is not.

I have no trouble believing that there is some sort of unknown ape or even human ancestor living in the wilderness of North America and especially in Canada. As I mentioned in my book *Canadian Monsters and Mysteries,* Canada is the second-largest country in the world, and something like ninety percent of its population lives within one hundred fifty miles of the border with the United States. This fact leaves vast areas of wilderness virtually uninhabited by human beings. Author Thomas Steenburg commented in an interview with *Monster-Quest* that the entire landmass of Europe would fit nicely in the wilderness of Canada with room to spare.

Such large wilderness areas leave open the possibility that unknown species may exist in the less travelled areas of the Great White North. A case in point is the wood bison, North America's largest animal by weight. The wood bison was declared extinct in the early 1900s, only to be rediscovered in Alberta in 1957.

When Esteban Sarmiento, a noted primatologist, undertook an environmental survey for *MonsterQuest*, he noted that the boreal forest environment where he did his survey contained a wide variety of food sources for a large primate. It is well known that Canada's wild areas support both black and brown bears, with brown bears approaching the supposed mass of a Sasquatch.

People in the wilds of Canada and beyond are seeing something, and I believe it is entirely possible that some Sasquatch are actually giant apes such as the economy-sized *Gigantopithecus blacki* from 350,000 years ago. After all, such a time period is a blink of the eye in geological terms. I see no reason not to think the creature may have survived.

However, even if there is a large primate wandering the forests of Canada and beyond, and even if researchers do eventually produce such an animal for scientific examination, that does not give researchers the right to simply ignore all evidence that does not fit into the flesh and blood hypothesis. People have had and continue to have markedly weird encounters with Sasquatch that bear examination.

Flesh and blood researchers strive so mightily to explain these strange occurrences that they seem to be willing to give the Sasquatch superhero-level powers in their effort to look away from paranormal explanations.

People experience shattering terror at the very sight of the creature? The animal uses infrasound as part of its hunting arsenal, just like a tiger.

Sasquatch simply vanishes before the witness' eyes? The creature has developed the ability to camouflage itself as a survival mechanism over the years.

The witness hears the creature speaking in his or her mind? The witness was overwrought and simply fantasized or imagined this event, or, perhaps, the witness is a little mentally unstable.

May all the gods forbid that one of these researchers look at a witness and say, "I don't know how that happened" and leave a mystery a mystery!

The flip-flopping continues when the flesh and blood

researcher, who lives for the discovery of Sasquatch tracks, finds a track or tracks that do not match expectations. The Fouke Monster of *Legend of Boggy Creek* fame in Arkansas was said to leave three-toed tracks, and the 2008 sighting of Helen Pahpasay in Ontario culminated in a six-toed track find. Conventional primatology does not admit of any number of toes on a primate but five. This leaves flesh and blood researchers to either deny that these tracks were made by a Sasquatch, or theorize that the tracks were hoaxed or in some way altered from their original appearance (melting snow, shifting soil, etc.). There has even been theorizing that such tracks come from creatures that have birth defects or other mutations.

While both/and thinking must allow that such ideas could be true, I think it is far simpler to look at these anomalous events surrounding Sasquatch from a more animistic perspective. As we reviewed in a previous section, many First Nations people understand that the Sasquatch is a real being, but they also feel that the creature is much more than another animal in the woods. Their understanding seems to be that the Hairy One exists in two worlds, our seemingly physical world and what I call the Otherworld, and that the creatures walk freely between those worlds.

Additionally, Native people seem to feel that, when the Sasquatch is in our realm, it is as solid as we are, capable of interacting physically with its environment. Thus, we have a cause for all the tracks, hair, and other physical traces in addition to the puzzling nature of some of that evidence. I am thinking specifically of trackways that lead out into open areas and then disappear or creatures that simply vanish in front of the witness.

While many researchers might roll their eyes and dismiss such conjectures as "woo", I come from a strongly animistic and magical background and have to give credence to folk, like the

First Nations people, who come from strongly animistic traditions. Animism is a complex subject, but, put simply, it is a belief that the seemingly physical world in which we dwell (which quantum physics tells us is not solid at all) is also inhabited by spirits. Many of the beings are attached to the land on which we and they live and the many features of that land.

While most of us cannot see these beings, for centuries there have been practitioners who can. These people are called many things in many cultures—shaman, medicine person, witch, magician—but they mostly agree that our world is a far stranger place than we have been led to believe by Western scientific materialism.

As noted with First Nations beliefs, there is a strong notion in animistic cultures that there are spirits who can walk back and forth between the worlds. I am most familiar with the faery of Celtic and Canadian lore, and "those ones" provide a good example.

In the lore, the faery people exist in a separate place, sometimes simply called Faery or given a euphemism such as "under the hills". Though they live apart from us, the faery are quite capable of moving into our world and interacting with humans, for good or ill, if they so choose. These interactions extend all the way up to mating with humans, so there can be no doubt that some, if not all, faery have a very physical existence when they are on our plane.

The faery, by themselves, compose a vast compendium of beings. The reader has only to look at a tome like Katharine Briggs' *An Encyclopedia of Fairies* to realize that these beings existed to people in various cultures throughout Europe and the world, and they existed in a wild variety of forms, many of which could bring themselves into our plane of reality.

But faery are not the only spirits that surround us. If the faery can bring themselves into our world, then why not a creature like Sasquatch? Such a supposition in no way denies the reality of these beings. They are here, witnesses are seeing them, and evidence is being left behind. The difference is that, when they accomplish whatever they set out to do on our plane, they can travel back to their own plane and become invisible, once more, to our eyes.

A Sasquatch of a spiritual nature could also help explain the prevalence of roadside sightings. As I noted in that section, roads of all kinds can be viewed as liminal areas and could be places where it is easier for spirits to slip from their world into ours. If we go completely down the rabbit hole and note that roads in the UK often track along what some researchers call ley lines, then the same might be true in Canada. A ley line is a track of geomantic energy and might provide needed power for the transition from one world to the next.

I realize that this is wild conjecture, but, if we are to make any headway in exploring these mysteries, I feel it is high time we started thinking outside the box.

If we accept that Sasquatch might have a spiritual nature, we are also able to understand incidents where the witness has been seized with extreme terror—there is a reason why magicians evoking spirits request that the spirit appear in a form that is not terrifying—or experienced what is sometimes called mind speak. After all, spirits have been communicating with shaman, mind to mind, for millennia.

The troublesome cases of Sasquatch disappearing in a flash of light can be accepted as simply true, and the anomalous lights that are often seen before or after a sighting can be seen as part of the overall event. Lights are associated with faery and ghosts, why not a world-walking Sasquatch? There is even the possibility that the lights represent the form of these creatures in their purest aspect.

So, alright, the reader might be saying, this writer feels that

Sasquatch are spirit creatures that move back and forth between what he calls the Otherworld and the physical dimension where we live.

Not exactly, what I am saying is that, exercising both/and thinking, both the flesh and blood hypothesis and the spirit hypothesis could be true. We should not, however, stop there. If we are going to truly set ourselves up in the hinterlands outside the proverbial box, we need to consider other theories as well.

It may be, for example, that some sightings of the Hairy One are psychic events. Psychic abilities have been demonstrated in double-blind laboratory trials over and over. Only someone completely unwilling to look at the experiments can come to any other conclusion. The experiments have also shown that psi works best when a person is in a relaxed state of mind, such as when they are out hiking in nature, spending a quiet day camping or fishing in a lake or stream.

If one were going to have a psychic event, then these are times when such an event might occur, and if the event occurs, then one of several things might be happening. The person experiencing psi might simply be seeing into what I call the Otherworld and seeing a creature—the Sasquatch—that lives on the Other Side and happens to be in the witness' area.

Conversely, the person might be using a clairvoyant talent that looks back in time so that he or she is viewing an extinct species that used to exist in our reality but is no longer extant. Finally, the experiencer might be seeing a spirit that his or her mind cannot translate into a recognizable perception. Sifting through its database, the Sasquatch may be the closest thing that the mind can come up with to what it is "actually" seeing.

In conjunction with the idea that Sasquatch may be creatures who can cross from our dimension into another is the idea that the forest giants may be moving not between dimensions but through time. We know that a giant ape was extant in China and could have made it across the Bering land bridge during the last ice age. Perhaps what people are seeing is not actually a relict example of *Gigantopithecus blacki*. Instead, it may be that these giant apes occasionally wander through as yet unexplained time distortions and end up in wilderness across the world. Again, this is wild conjecture on my part, but I want to make the point that there are lots of ways to think about this phenomenon once we take the blinkers off, and any or all of them could be true.

There are, of course, other theories about Sasquatch. Greg and Dana Newkirk, of *Hellier* fame, offered the idea on a *Finding Bigfoot* episode that experiencers were seeing the ghost of an ancient hominid. People who are attracted by the Sasquatch and UFO sightings have speculated that Sasquatch is an alien species brought here by the UFO occupants for mysterious reasons. Those who have read my other books know that I am not a huge fan of the extraterrestrial hypothesis, but I include this idea for the sake of thoroughness.

Additionally, there are biblically oriented theorists who think that Sasquatch might be the result of matings between fallen angels and humans, the so-called Nephilim. I personally think this is a misinterpretation of the Books of Enoch, but I include the idea for those interested in further research.

If we open our minds, set aside our pet theory, and really set ourselves the task of examining Sasquatch, all we can say is that we do not know what Sasquatch is but that there are a world of possibilities. I have said, on many occasions, that those who study cryptids and the paranormal need to have a high tolerance for mystery.

That word mystery derives from Greek, muein, and once had a meaning of keeping the eyes or mouth shut. It was used for those who were initiated into certain ritual occasions (such as the Eleusinian Mysteries) and could not, thereafter, speak of them on pain of death. It is also related to the word mystic with its connotations of an individual seeking union with a Higher Source.

Maybe, instead of arguing about who is right and who is wrong in this field of so many options, we should allow ourselves to be taken up in the mystery of Sasquatch and allow that mystery to open our eyes to a wider world. It might just be that, as researchers like Mike Clelland have suggested, these close encounters with mystery are initiatic experiences. Since we in the West no longer have the intense rites of passage seen in earlier cultures, the experience of Sasquatch or other mysteries may be the thing that causes a death to our old life and rebirth into a new life.

Bibliography: Books

Bord, Janet, and Colin Bord. *Alien animals*. Stackpole Books, 1980.

Bord, Janet and Colin. *Modern Mysteries of the World*. Grafton Books, 1989.

Briggs, Katharine Mary. *An Encyclopedia of Fairies: Hobgoblins, Brownies, Bogies, and Other Supernatural Creatures*. Pantheon, 1976.

Childress, David H. *Bigfoot Nation: The History of Sasquatch in North America*. Adventures Unlimited Press, 2018.

Clelland, Mike. *The Messengers: Owls, Synchronicity, and the UFO Abductee*. Richard Dolan Press, 2020.

Coleman, Loren. *The Field Guide to Bigfoot, Yeti, and Other Mystery Primates Worldwide*. Avon Books, 1999.

De Becker, Gavin. *The Gift of Fear: Listening to the Intuition that Protects Us from Danger*. Little, Brown & Company, 1997.

Dennett, Preston. *Bigfoot, Yeti, and Other Ape-Men.* Chelsea House, 2008.

Evans-Wentz, Walter Yeeling. *The Fairy Faith in Celtic Countries: The Classic Study of Leprechauns, Pixies, and Other Fairy Spirits.* Citadel Press, 2003.

Gerhard, Ken. *The Essential Guide to Bigfoot.* Beyond the Fray Publishing, 2019.

Marjorie Halpin and Michael Ames, eds., 1980. *Manlike Monsters on Trial.* University of British Columbia Press, from Michael Taft, "Sasquatch-like Creatures in Newfoundland: A Study in the Problems of Belief, Perception and Reportage."

Hunter, Don, and Dahinden, Rene. *Sasquatch.* New American Library, 1975.

Hynes, Bruce. *Here Be Dragons: Strange Creatures of Newfoundland and Labrador.* Breakwater Books, 2012.

Merrick, Elliot. *True North.* Heron Dance Press, 2005.

Moskowitz-Strain, Kathy. *Giants, Cannibals and Monsters: Bigfoot in Native Culture.* Hancock House, UK ed., 2020.

Ogden, Tom. *The Complete Idiot's Guide to Ghosts and Hauntings.* Alpha Books, 1999.

Renner, Timothy, and Cutchin, Joshua. *Where the Footprints End, Vol 1 & 2.* Dark Holler Arts, 2020.

Sanderson, Ivan T. *Abominable Snowmen, Legend Come to Life.* Cosimo, Inc., 2007.

Steenburg, Thomas. *Sasquatch in Alberta.* Hancock House Publishers Ltd., 2018.

Warms, John. *Strange Creatures Seldom Seen: Giant Beavers, Sasquatch, Manipogos, and Other Mystery Animals in Manitoba and Beyond.* PDF format, publication date not cited.

Watson, W. T. *Canadian Monsters and Mysteries.* Beyond the Fray Publishing, 2022.

Watson, W. T. *Mysteries in the Mist: Mist, Fog and Clouds in the Paranormal.* Beyond the Fray Publishing, 2022.

Watson, W. T. *Phantom Black Dogs: Walkers of the Liminal Way*. Beyond the Fray Publishing, 2021.

Wilson, Colin. *Poltergeist: A Classic Study in Destructive Hauntings*. Llewellyn Worldwide, 2010.

BIBLIOGRAPHY: INTERNET/VIDEO

Bibliography: Internet and Video Sources

Barlow, Scott. "Near Waterton National Park, Alberta, Canada". Bigfoot Encounters, 07 January 2003. http://bigfootencounters.com

Beachcombing. "Strange Labrador Monster". Beachcombing's Bizarre History Blog. 28 August 2016. http://www.strangehistory.net/2016/08/28/strange-labrador-monster/

Beleutz, Curt. "Algonquin National Park, Ontario, Canada, 1999". Bigfoot Encounters. 03 February 2000. http://bigfootencounters.com

Bellamy, Robin P. "Manitoba Man Claims Sasquatch Sighting". Sasquatch Canada, uncited date. https://www.sasquatchcanada.com/manitoba-sightings.html

Bernbaum, Brian. "The Odd Truth: Bigfoot sighted in Yukon". CBS News, 14 June 2004. https://www.cbsnews.com/news/the-odd-truth-june-11-2004/

Coleman, Loren. "New Ontario Sasquatch Track Find". Cryptomundo, 26 July 2008. http://cryptomundo.com/cryptozoo-news/sasq-kenora/

211

Couture, Roger. "Report to SasquatchCanada". Sasquatch-Canada, 11 February 2017. https://www.sasquatchcanada.com/quebec-sightings.html

Cundiff, Vic, host. "Witness: Chris". *Bigfoot Eyewitness Radio*, Episode 191, 27 August 2019.

Cundiff, Vic, host. "Witness: Sean". *Bigfoot Eyewitness Radio*, Episode 239, 7 July 2020.

Forker, Sean, et al, host. "Canadian Bigfoot Encounters". *Sasquatch Experience*, Episode 10, 9 October 2020.

Germer, Wes. "A Man Describes His Encounter with a Nàhga". Sasquatch Chronicles Blog, 02 April 2020. https://sasquatchchronicles.com/a-man-canada-describes-his-encounter-with-a-nahgạ/

Germer, Wes, host. "Do Not Chase Strange Lights". *Sasquatch Chronicles Podcast*, Episode 191, 07 February 2016.

Germer, Wes, host. "I Shouldn't Be Alive". *Sasquatch Chronicles Podcast*, Episode 515, 15 February 2019.

Germer, Wes. "It's Face Was Literally Something Out of Hell". Sasquatch Chronicles Blog, 22 March 2019. https://sasquatchchronicles.com/its-face-was-literally-something-out-of-hell/

Germer, Wes. "Listener Shares Encounter from Manitoba Canada". Sasquatch Chronicles Blog, 04 October 2016. https://sasquatchchronicles.com/listener-shares-encounter-from-manitoba-canada/

Germer, Wes. "Manitoba Bigfoot Encounter". Sasquatch Chronicles Blog, 15 December 2017. https://sasquatchchronicles.com/sc-ep389-manitoba-bigfoot-encounter/

Germer, Wes, host. "The Face was Human Like Only Bigger and Wider". *Sasquatch Chronicles Podcast*, Episode 298, 12 February 2017.

Germer, Wes, host. "The Snelgrove Lake Incident". *Sasquatch Chronicles Podcast*. Episode 312, 03 April 2017.

Germer, Wes. "What Looked At Us That Day Was More Ape Than Man". Sasquatch Chronicles Blog. 14 March 2017. https://sasquatchchronicles.com/what-looked-at-us-that-day-was-more-ape-than-man/

Grossinger, Red. "Report to SasquatchCanada". Sasquatch-Canada, uncited date. https://www.sasquatchcanada.com/yukon-sightings.html

Hajicek, Doug, creator. "Sasquatch Attacks". *Monster Quest*, Season 1, Episode 2, History Channel/Whitewolf Entertainment, 7 Nov. 2007, Accessed 22 July 2022.

Hajicek, Doug, creator. "Sasquatch Attacks II". *Monster Quest*, Season 2, Episode 17, History Channel/Whitewolf Entertainment, 12 Nov. 2008, Accessed 22 July 2022.

Heibert, D. "Temagami Bigfoot". SasquatchCanada.com. 15 April 2009. https://www.sasquatchcanada.com/ontario-sightings.html

Johnson, Frank. "Marsh Monster Exists". *Thorburn Post*, 5 August 1913. Imaged by SasquatchCanada. https://www.sasquatchcanada.com/nova-scotia-sightings.html

Knox, Shawn. "Fun Friday; Bigfoot sighting in Saskatchewan?". Global News. 24 January 2014. https://globalnews.ca/news/1105882/fun-friday-bigfoot-sighting-in-saskatchewan/

Michael, Allex. "Late At Night". Bigfoot Encounters. June 1996. http://bigfootencounters.com

Nelson, Curt. "Unusual Sasquatch". *SasquatchCanada Virtual Magazine*, uncited date. https://www.sasquatchcanada.com/uploads/9/4/5/1/945132/unusual_sasquatch.pdf

"New Brunswick, Canada Bigfoot Sighting". YouTube, uploaded by Canadian Bigfoot Research Organization, 05 October 2020.

No cited author. "Amazing Stories Elders Pass Down". Alberta Sasquatch: Bigfoot in the Canadian Rockies blog. 14

May 2018. https://sasquatchalberta.com/indigenous-outlook/1772/

No cited author. "Berry-pickers report sasquatch sighting in Northern Ontario". CBC News, 28 July 2008. https://www.cbc.ca/news/canada/manitoba/berry-pickers-report-sasquatch-sighting-in-northern-ontario-1.762011

No cited author. "Bigfoot sighting reported by Cree hunter near Wemindji, Que." CBC, 29 August 2013. https://www.cbc.ca/news/canada/montreal/bigfoot-sighting-reported-by-cree-hunter-near-wemindji-que-1.1371794

No cited author. "Drumming Chimps and the Wood Knocking Connection". Texas Cryptid Hunter, 31 January 2015. http://texascryptidhunter.blogspot.com/2015/01/drumming-chimps-and-wood-knocking.html

No cited author. "Interview with a Sasquatch Researcher". Alberta Sasquatch: Bigfoot in the Canadian Rockies blog. 14 May 2018. https://sasquatchalberta.com/indigenous-outlook/interview-with-an-indigenous-sasquatch-researcher/

No cited author. "Sasquatch Sighting by Nunavik Berry Pickers". CBC News, 04 Oct. 2012. https://www.cbc.ca/news/canada/north/sasquatch-sighting-by-nunavik-berry-pickers-1.1164008

Roger, Lynn, PhD. "How Dangerous are Black Bears?". North American Bear Center, uncited date. https://bear.org/how-dangerous-are-black-bears/

Rosales, Albert. "1969-Canada". UFOInfo.com. Uncited Date. https://www.ufoinfo.com/humanoid/humanoid1969.shtml

Richey, Stephen, L. (submitted). "Yukon Men Convinced They Saw a Sasquatch". BFRO Media Article #389, 10 June 2004. https://www.bfro.net/GDB/show_article.asp?id=389

Sasquatch'n. YouTube, uploaded by Animiki See Distribution, 15 September 2020.

Sasquatch on Lake Superior. YouTube, uploaded by Dee McCullay (Dark History/Thunderstryker Films), 01 August 2017.

Scott, Edward. "The Boogeyman". Bigfoot Encounters. 15 January 2012. http://bigfootencounters.com

Sinclair, Kristi Lane. "On the Legend of the Sasquatch". *Sequi*. No date cited. https://sesqui.ca/en/news/kristi-lane-sinclair-on-the-legend-of-the-sasquatch/

Steer, Bill. "Are there sasquatches in the back roads?". Sootoday.com. 26 January 2022. https://www.sootoday.com/columns/back-roads-bill/are-there-sasquatches-on-the-back-roads-4998013?utm_source=sudbury.com&utm_campaign=sudbury.com%3A%20outbound&utm_medium=referral

Steer, Bill. "Following Further in the footsteps of Sasquatch". Sudbury.com, 2 February 2022. https://www.sudbury.com/local-news/following-further-in-the-footsteps-of-sasquatch-5022753

Strickler, Lon. "Bigfoot in New Brunswick Canada". Phantoms and Monsters, 13 September 2019. https://www.phantomsandmonsters.com/2019/09/bigfoot-carrying-deer-brazos-river-hood.html

Strickler, Lon. "Newfoundland Bigfoot". Phantoms and Monsters, 28 June 2016. https://www.phantomsandmonsters.com/2016/06/newfoundland-bigfoot.html

Tarnowetski, Robin. "Bigfoot: Real or Myth?". SaskToday. 22 October 2014. https://www.sasktoday.ca/north/opinion/bigfoot-real-or-myth-4068493

"The Craven Bigfoot Footage". Youtube, uploaded by The Chase - Funniest Moments, 20 January 2014.

"The Traverspine Gorilla: A Wildman Story from Labrador, Canada". YouTube, uploaded by Hammerson Peters, 28 January 2021.

Therriault, Ednor. "Call it Yeti, Wendigo, Chuchuna or

Sasquatch, you'd better believe there are believers". Mountain Outlaw, uncited date. https://www.mtoutlaw.com/in-search-of-bigfoot/

Viala, Sean. "The Lake Minnewanka Wildman". *Sasquatch-Canada Virtual Magazine*, uncited date. https://www.sasquatchcanada.com/uploads/9/4/5/1/945132/lake_minnewanka_wildman.pdf

Witness: Anonymous. "ASO Report 041 - Visual Account in Waterton on the Akamina Parkway". Alberta Sasquatch, 22 February 2018. https://sasquatchalberta.com/reports/aso-report-041-visual-encounter-in-waterton-on-the-akamina-parkway/

Witness: Anonymous. "ASO Report #060 - Witness had Terrifying Encounter Near Slave Lake". Alberta Sasquatch, 14 December 2020. https://sasquatchalberta.com/reports/aso-report-060-witness-has-terrifying-encounter-near-slave-lake/

Witness: Anonymous. "ASO Report 065 - A Brief Sighting West of Little Smoky". Alberta Sasquatch, 14 December 2020. https://sasquatchalberta.com/reports/aso-report-065-a-brief-sighting-west-of-little-smoky/

Witness: Anonymous. "ASO Report #066 - Special Forces Soldier had dramatic Wainwright Encounter". Alberta Sasquatch, 26 June 2019. https://sasquatchalberta.com/reports/aso-report-066-special-forces-soldier-has-dramatic-wainwright-encounter/

Witness: Anonymous. "Report #7139". Bigfoot Field Researchers Organization. 19 October 2003. https://www.bfro.net/GDB/show_report.asp?id=7139

Witness: Anonymous. "Report #10611". Bigfoot Field Researchers Organization. 12 February 2005. https://www.bfro.net/GDB/show_report.asp?id=10611

Witness: Anonymous. "Report #12733". Bigfoot Field

Researchers Organization. 6 October 2005. https://www.bfro.
net/GDB/show_report.asp?id=12733

Witness: Anonymous. "Report #13061". Bigfoot Field
Researchers Organization. 16 November 2005. https://www.
bfro.net/GDB/show_report.asp?id=13061

Witness: Anonymous. "Report #15343". Bigfoot Field
Researchers Organization. 27 July 2006. http://www.bfro.net/
gdb/show_report.asp?id=15343

Witness: Anonymous. "Report #17221". Bigfoot Field
Researchers Organization. 6 January 2007. http://www.bfro.
net/GDB/show_report.asp?id=17221

Witness: Anonymous. "Report #23171". Bigfoot Field
Researchers Organization. 14 February 2008. https://www.
bfro.net/GDB/show_report.asp?id=23171

Witness: Anonymous. "Report #31992". Bigfoot Field
Researchers Organization. 10 January 2012. https://www.bfro.
net/GDB/show_report.asp?id=31992

Witness: Anonymous. "Report to SasquatchCanada".
SasquatchCanada, 22 February 2013. https://www.sasquatch
canada.com/quebec-sightings.html

Witness: Bill. "Report #16779". Bigfoot Field Researchers
Organization. 27 November 2006. https://www.bfro.net/
GDB/show_report.asp?id=16779

Witness: DJ. "Report #1281". Bigfoot Field Researchers
Organization. 15 July 1998. https://www.bfro.net/GDB/
show_report.asp?id=1281

Witness: DP. "Report #12335". Bigfoot Field Researchers
Organization. 15 July 1998. https://www.bfro.net/GDB/
show_report.asp?id=12335

Witness: Anonymous. "Report #14405". Bigfoot Field
Researchers Organization. 17 April 2006. https://www.bfro.
net/GDB/show_report.asp?id=14405

Witness: Druery, Richard, and Krick, Margie. "Report

#1340". Bigfoot Field Researchers Organization. 17 November 1997. https://www.bfro.net/GDB/show_report.asp?id=1340

Witness: Manley, Liz. "Report #65338". Bigfoot Field Researchers Organization. 23 March 2020. https://www.bfro.net/GDB/show_report.asp?id=65238

Witness: Warren, Desmond. "Report #1291". Bigfoot Field Researchers Organization. 01 July 1998. https://www.bfro.net/GDB/show_report.asp?id=1291

Witness: Earl. "Report to SasquatchCanada". Sasquatch-Canada, 26 March 2013. https://www.sasquatchcanada.com/nova-scotia-sightings.html

Witness: "J". "Lake Christie, Ottawa, Ontario, Canada". Bigfoot Encounters. 26 March 2004. http://bigfootencounters.com.

Witness: John D. "Red Deer, Alberta Incident 2005 (Canada)". Bigfoot Encounters, uncited date. http://bigfootencounters.com.

Witness: Peter. "Report #9552". Bigfoot Field Researchers Organization, 16 October 2004. https://www.bfro.net/GDB/show_report.asp?id=9552

Witness: Steve D. "Report 7353". Bigfoot Field Researchers Organization, 8 November 2003. https://www.bfro.net/GDB/show_report.asp?id=7353

Bibliography: Newspapers and Periodicals

Frazier, Joe. "Some Doubt, Some Believe, Some Aren't Sure." *The Daily Herald-Tribune* (Grand Prairie, Alberta), 26 November 1975.

Loran, Tom. "Is It a Great Hairy Beast or a Myth That Won't Die?" *Edmonton Journal*, 31 August 1974.

Nearingburg, Alison. "Sasquatch Reported, 44 Years Later." *Edmonton Journal*, 12 May 1982.

No cited author. "Abominable Experience." *Red Deer Advocate*, 13 May 1974.

No cited author. "It's Not a Bear, It's not a Moose - It's a Sasquatch, Yukoners Swear." *Ottawa Citizen*, 20 July 2005.

No cited author. "Saskatchewan Woman Spots Bigfoot." *Edmonton Journal*, 15 December 2006.

No cited author. "Sasquatch Sighting Reported." *The Expositor* (Brantford, Ontario), 19 August 1982.

Ryan, Mary. "The Royal Canadian Mounted Police at Vancouver". *Flying Saucer Review*. 18 July 1973.

Stone, Peter. "Time Stood Still; My Expression Was Awe". *Whitehorse Daily Star*, 22 July 2005.

Warren, Jeremy. "Woman Claims Sasquatch Sighting." *Star-Phoenix* (Saskatoon, Saskatchewan), 15 December 2006.

ABOUT THE AUTHOR

Amazon best-selling author W. T. Watson is a coffee addict and writer of both fiction and non-fiction. He infuses his work with his expertise in cryptozoology, monster lore, magic, Forteana and the paranormal. W.T. brings a unique shamanic and magical perspective to all of his work after over 30 years of exploration in these topics. When he is not writing or reading about monsters, he can be found outdoors allowing his dogs to take him for a walk around his neighbourhood in Kitchener, Ontario. He lives with his spouse, Stacey, in a townhome that would be jammed with books if it weren't for e-readers.

facebook.com/blackdog60

twitter.com/WTWatson2

instagram.com/curunir60

Hunting The Beast: A Novel

Phantom Black Dogs: Walkers of the Liminal Way

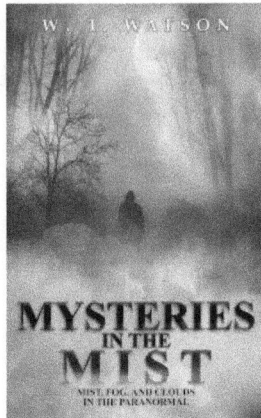

Mysteries in the Mist: Mist, Fog, and Clouds in the Paranormal

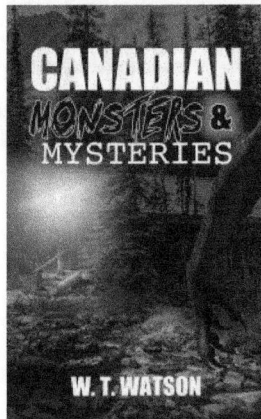

Canadian Monsters & Mysteries

www.ingramcontent.com/pod-product-compliance
Lightning Source LLC
Chambersburg PA
CBHW032348280326
41935CB00008B/495